HANDBOOK GUIDE TO CONSULTATIVE SALES

by

J. Michael Smith

Illustrated by

David Myers

For Xander, Connor, Zoey, Sara Kate, & Lauren.

"Tirelessly search for the wonder and wisdom the world has to offer. And when you find it, share it with everyone you meet."

To my soulmate, friend, and partner in this life, Brooke:

"Thank you. I could not have done any of this without your support. You will always be the best proof I have that this guy can sell!"

Table of Contents

Chapter 1: Why Consultative Selling? 4

Chapter 2: The Loadout 18

Chapter 3: Breaking Biology 42

Chapter 4: Conscientious Leadership 58

Chapter 5: Assessment 82

Chapter 6: Analysis 109

Chapter 7: Summary Report Prep & Presentation 128

Chapter 8: In Closing 154

References 157

About 158

Chapter One

Why Consultative Selling?

Let's talk about you.

Chances are, there's an aspect of your role defined by marketing your products and services to others. You have a clearly defined picture of who needs your products and services. You know how it improves their personal or professional lives. You are acutely aware of how you benefit from each sale. But somewhere there is a disconnect. You may feel there can be an improvement. Or you may feel uncertain as how to connect to your market. One thing is certain, however – traditional sales is not cutting it by itself.

Whether you're looking to start sales, break through a sales plateau, or add another arrow to your already impressive sales quiver: this handbook is for you. This brief guide is designed to provide you with the tools necessary to flip the traditional sales paradigm on its head and revolutionize the way your potential customers view your approach. Notice who the emphasis is on in that previous sentence. It is all about the customer. Different already, right? That difference connects to the very heart of Consultative Sales. But before we go there, let's consider the traditional sales model.

Traditional Sales-Model:

Here is a familiar scenario. Gung-ho sales person with resilient belief in their products and services sets off on an approach to knock down every door, ring every phone, light up every inbox and social media blast the hell out of their assigned territory. Why? Because somewhere along in their training, someone with authority told them, "It's a numbers game." With that sage advice came a formula that went something like:

"If you make 100 calls each day, 40 of those calls will pick up the phone. Of those 40 calls, 8 people will express interest in your product or service. Of those 8 people, 4 will set a meeting with you. And of those 4, statistically 1 will become a customer."

So, all you have to do is make 1 customer a day and multiply that by the average sale price to calculate your commission and if you do that every day of the week, look at how much you will earn. Then, they introduce you to some old dude who is their top sales guy and you are instantly mesmerized that this sales guy put in that kind of work. Then, that good old sales person's ego kicks in and you begin to think that if this curmudgeon represents their best; just imagine what you can do!

Sales people are traditionally competitive, driven and live for that "high" that can only come from a wet signature on a new sale. This vigor can sometimes come across as pushy or disingenuous. It is the largest and often the only attributable cause for any negative connotation surrounding the word "sales." And ironically, it begins with the way sales is approached.

In the traditional sales model, it is the role of the sales person to bring their product or service to the customer. And, they are told to do so with a blind disregard of the customer's situation. After all, it's just a numbers game, right? And this is where the disconnect begins. In the deepest part of our human nature, we believe in the significant worth of others. The highest rewards and accolades are set aside for those who do the most for humanity. The worst punishment is set aside for those who do the worst to humanity. So, to enter into any field where human interaction is boiled down to a "numbers game" is in direct conflict with our inherent morality. (Right here, people are either agreeing enthusiastically or defensively prepping their argument for why the numbers game works. If you recall, it was never mentioned that it didn't work. It just creates some unnecessary issues, and it most certainly doesn't work for everyone.)

Plus, in the world of Google and Amazon, if you want it, you can go find it. A decision maker doesn't really need someone showing up unexpectedly offering something they haven't already bothered to look for on their own. This is drastically different from the sales world prior to the digital information age. It used to be that they needed a "guy for that." So, all you had to do was let them know you sold the things they needed a "guy" for, then provide service to the account and it was yours for decades.

Consider the old sales pro mentioned previously. Gray hair and hemorrhoids aren't the only things he's got. He's got customers. Loads of them. He doesn't spend his time making 100 calls a day. As a matter of fact, he works less than anyone in the entire organization. But he's invaluable because his customers love him. And THEY CALL HIM! What a mind-blowing paradox that is. The number one sales person in the entire company is the number one person because his phone rings. Not because he's dutifully ringing every phone in the MSA. This happens because he knows them. He knows their organization and the people in it. He knows the decision makers. He knows who they are, what they do, what they have and therefore he already knows what they need.

Here's a question for your consideration. If you know the needs of decision makers have shifted because of the information age, and you know that you would LOVE to have the kind of customers and sales numbers the old pro has; WHY would anyone instruct you to get there by doing things contrary to what you just established to be true?

Maybe you shouldn't.

Consultative Sales Model:

In the Traditional Sales Model, your goal is to focus on Products and Services. Training encompasses learning everything there is to know about your organizations marketable output so that when the time comes for you to market to your territory, you can answer any question and overcome any objection (which may even include the Customer's belief they do not need it).

The Consultative Sales Model literally flips that paradigm on its head. It is backwards from the Traditional Sales Model. Traditionally, a marketer or sales person represents the Product or Service and brings it to the Customer. But in the Consultative Sales Model, the sales person represents the Customer and brings them to the appropriate Products and Services you offer.

This simple, but significant shift does not change the overall role of the sales person. You still have to get out there and find Customers who are in need of your organization's products and services. But it is designed to drastically change your perspective on how to get there. It places the focus where it belongs – on the Customer. It redirects your approach from a traditional sales representative, to that of a consultant.

The irony is that both practitioners require the same skill sets to successfully execute their roles.

QUALITIES OF A PROFESSIONAL:

SALES PERSON	CONSULTANT
• Leadership	• Leadership
• Sympathy / Empathy	• Sympathy / Empathy
• Critical Thinking Skills	• Analytical Thinking
• Problem Solving	• Problem Solving
• Planning	• Planning
• Interpersonal Communication	• Interpersonal Communication

The consultant pursues a course of action not typically associated by the world at large with someone in "sales." The sales cycle for a consultant isn't about burning through potential contacts on a time-sensitive quest to find an immediate buyer. Instead, it is about making the assumption that anyone in your target market should eventually become one. So, the challenge is to deepen a relationship with a customer based upon THEIR NEED to for a solution rather than slaying them with fact-benefit selling until they align a benefit with their perceived needs. In fact, this can all be boiled down to customer expectations. Any decision maker being called on by a sales representative expects to be sold to. Any decision maker being addressed by a consultant expects to be presented solutions to their issues (whether known or unknown) based upon detailed analysis.

As a consultant, you are expected to provide assessment, analysis and then ...solutions. How do those solutions present themselves to you, the consultant? In the form of answers and assessment of the customer's past, present and future. How do these solutions present themselves to the customer? In the form of products and services offered by your organization as marketable output designed to meet the now well-known needs of the customer.

Imagine a sales appointment where you're not laser focused on getting someone to agree to something. Instead, you're allowing yourself to express genuine curiosity about them, their organization, and their current and future needs. That's consulting.

"In Consultative Sales, it is not your job to be the smartest person in the room. It's your job to be the most curious."

Here's why that matters:

- **It reduces burnout** – Sales at 100 or even 50 cold calls a day is exhausting! Most people will tell you that is why the average turnover rate for sales professionals is 35% (Forbes, Comaford 2016). That means organizations with 10 reps are replacing 3 of them each year. In a 2019 survey conducted by Hubspot, 68% of all sales people describe their lifestyle as challenging and 54% add the word stressful to that!

- **It creates larger sales** – In 2017, a 50 year-old B2B Company's average sale was just above $5,000 with revenues hovering around $4 million. In 2018, they implemented the Consultative Sales Method. By mid-year of 2019, their average sale had more than doubled, and their first major Consultative Sale reached into the six-figure mark. Plus they got paid to tell the organization what to buy from them! In 2019, their revenues had climbed to $6 million.

- **It is HOW large organizations want to be sold to.** – 82% of B2B decision makers think sales reps are unprepared and 65% of buyers come away from the sales process frustrated by the experience. So, good luck setting appointments with decision makers at organizations with large market caps by calling with a pitch! Statistically, the larger the organization, the slower the turnover rate in their vendor relationships. Yet these organizations represent the ideal customer for most marketers. And, a few large customers can often replace revenue from tens or even hundreds of smaller relationships. The

Consultative Sales approach has been proven effective in reaching decision makers at large organizations.

- **It overcomes the "If I need it, I will find it" decisionmaker mentality** – "According to research from CEB, the average B2B buyer is at least 57% through a purchase decision before ever connecting with a sales person. This means sellers need to engage with prospects very differently – selling in a way that maps to the buyer's journey and expectations." (Forbes, Comaford 2016)

- **It puts you in a different category than other sales people** – Want to sell something? Find a way to stand out. According to data from Statista, US businesses will spend $197.47 billion on marketing in 2019. As a side note, those same businesses will spend less than half that amount training their frontline sales people in a similar way their competitors train. (Training Magazine, 2018 Industry Report) Training that exceeds expectations has proven to be 80.3% more effective in providing reps the tools to differentiate themselves in their respective markets!

- **It aligns with intrinsic ethical standards** – While there are a few sales people who can sleep at night having sold something to someone because they coaxed them into a decision; most get at least some twinge of guilt over pushing a product at someone.
- **It opens doors** – Interestingly, while it may be difficult to convince a business owner to open their door for a sales person; approximately 70% of small businesses hire consultants. (LinkedIn, 2018 Workforce Report)
- **It closes sales** – The Brevit Group posted a staggering statistic that only 13% of buyers believe sales people understand their needs. Infuse that statement with the fact that 71% of decision makers shop with a specific scenario, rather than a specific product, in mind (Compare Metrics, 2014). This is called a "needs scenario." And, ALL (yes, all) customers have at least one needs scenario! Therefore, if you can earn understanding of the client's situation; you can lead them to the appropriate products and services that accomplish their needs scenario(s).

- **It creates "sticky" relationships** – Did you know it costs an organization 5 times as much to earn a new customer as it does to retain a current one? A 2017 study by the Harvard Business Review involved what decision makers look for from their sales people. The results revealed that 40% of study participants prefer a salesperson who listens, understands, and then matches their solution to solve a specific problem. Another 30% prefer a salesperson who earns their trust by making them feel comfortable, because they will take care of the customer's long-term needs. Another 30% want a salesperson who challenges their thoughts and perceptions and then prescribes a solution that they may not have known about. The practice of Consultative Selling encompasses each of those aspects. How good would it feel to be 100% of what your decision makers are looking for?

Throughout the next 7 Chapters, this Handbook Guide to Consultative Sales will provide you with proven methods that lead to:

- larger sales
- more referrals
- more lines of business per customer
- turnkey replacement sales
- deeply entrenched customers
- increased sales confidence
- ease of approach

Each chapter is divided into 3 primary sections. The first section is a carefully crafted story designed to reveal the heart of the subject matter for that specific chapter. Some stories are funny, some are inspiring. But each carries a meaning beyond the surface-value of the story, itself – although that part is supposed to be fun too! The middle section is the meat of the chapter and includes references, statistics, and tips; while introducing you to the concept of Consultative Sales. Since this book is intended to be used as a guide, the last part of each chapter includes short bullet-point references for the subject matter contained in the chapter, and the layout is open and spacious to allow your own notes to be incorporated into your book. After all, this journey is about you!

Enjoy it!

Chapter One : Key Points

- In the Traditional Sales Model, the Sales Person represents the Product/Service and brings the Product/Service to the Customer
- In the Consultative Sales Model, the Sales Person represents the Customer and brings the Customer to the Product/Service
- Focus is placed where it belongs – on the Customer
- Redirects your approach from Sales Representative to that of a Consultant
- Qualities of Professional Consultants: Leadership, Sympathy/Empathy, Analytical Thinking, Problem Solving, Planning, Interpersonal Communication
- Make the assumption that every opportunity within your target market can become a customer
- Relationships are deepened based on organizational needs
- Decision makers addressed by consultants expect to be presented solutions to their issues based on detailed analysis
- "It's not your job to be the smartest person in the room, it's your job to be the most curious.

Chapter 2

The Load Out

"What's that one called, Papa?" His grandson, Charlie, pointed a small finger to the purple heart medal in its case. Mike looked at Charlie's bright blue eyes staring back at him with wonder while he curiously fumbled through his cigar box of US Army memorabilia. The four-year-old loved to pilfer through his Papa's pictures, medals, and memories kept from his time serving during the Korean War.

"That's the one you earn when you pay attention, so you only get shot a little bit." Mike chuckled.

"I wanna' see it." Charlie begged, eagerly crossing his fingers in front of his chest as if he were praying.

"Oh kiddo, I love you but..."

"Pleeeeeeease?" Charlie tilted his head as his eyes pleaded harder than his voice did.

"Ha! Alright, alright. You win, kid." Mike said, leaning over to ruffle Charlie's blonde hair with his fingers. "Us Papas can only resist so much of that."

He leaned over and pulled his right pant leg up to his knee, revealing two purple patches of skin. "Still there after all these years." He thought to himself.

"Is that where they shooted you, Papa?" Charlie asked, gently touching the scars on his grandfather's shin with the tip of his finger.

"That's it, kiddo." Mike replied. "But that's all they got!"

Mike lowered his pant leg and locked eyes with his grandson. "And now..." he brought his hands up beside his face, his fingers curled to mimic claws. Charlie began to giggle. "Now, I'm gonna' get you!" Mike gave a menacing glance and began tickling his grandson hysterically.

All his life, those two scars were a daily reminder of the importance of preparation. The day he got them, he listened to the most important speech of his life. And it lasted for about 2 minutes. They called it a "load out." His platoon leader, Sgt. Grimm – they called him Reaper – stood in front of a map with a long metal pointer.

"Gentlemen, we're going to roll up here, along the edge of this tree line. There's about a 20-degree incline through some thick cover and then it opens up into about a 3-acre clearing. Some of our best Recon men risked their lives to make sure you had access to the information I'm about to share with you, so don't piss on them by not listening!

"This kind of intel is the difference between soldiers who go home and bag their dames, and those who go home in bags to their dames. Got it?"

"Yes sir!" the platoon replied in thunderous voices.

Reaper went on to share the exact location of each known enemy position in the area, their estimated numbers, and what they were packing. He briefed them on where each M35 deuce-and-a-half soft-transport vehicle would stop and what to expect in terms of air support for the mission. Mike was assigned to M35 #6. The 2.5 ton truck; which is where its name comes from, would hold he and about 23 other members of his platoon.

The good news is they were flanked by a supporting gun-truck. The bad news is that meant their job was to take out the Soviet KPV heavy machine gun buried behind a bunker and protected by about 25 heavily-armed, Russian-trained KPA soldiers. Without overtaking the KPV, air support would be difficult. The terrain dictated that their truck was to approach from behind the hill. In a perfect world, the element of surprise would be on their side and the op would go smoothly. But, two months into his tour, Mike knew the only smooth operation to be had in Korea typically happened after eating a spicy fish-cake dish from a local street food vendor.

After the loadout, Mike passed by the topographic map on his way to the truck and noticed a rocky outcrop in the map drawing on the front side of the hill. If #6 was forced to change directions for any reason (the KPA notoriously blocked roads and set up traps to detour convoys, creating ambush scenarios) their unit could drop next to the outcrop and it would provide some additional cover.

"Hop on, son." Grimm said as he approached the large olive green transport. "Mind if I tag along? Looks like your unit's going to have all the fun taking out that nasty KPV." Reaper let out a raspy laugh as he clapped Mike on the back and shoved him up the metal step onto the rumbling truck full of soldiers.

He watched Reaper skillfully board the vehicle with the countenance of someone jumping into a truck headed into a field to do some farm labor. He lowered himself into the seat next to Mike, pulled a chewed cigar from his chest pocket and placed it in his mouth. "Mrs. Grimm asked me to stop smoking these before my last tour. So, now I don't light them anymore." He chuckled. "I'm a 24 year enlisted soldier headed into a war zone to kick down some Commies and I'm worried about what my wife thinks." Reaper shook his head. "How 'bout that, son?" He rolled the cigar to the side of his mouth. "What about you, Private? You got a special lady back home?"

"Yes, sir. Prettiest girl in Wyoming." Mike replied.

"Only girl in Wyoming." Reaper quipped. They both laughed.

"Sir?" Mike asked.

"What's that, Private?"

"Did you notice the rocky outcrop on the map to the West side of our drop point?"

"Hmmm... don't think so." The weathered old Sergeant's face wrinkled in thought.

"I think it might be a good place to drop, sir. Especially if we lose the element of surprise."

"Private, this mission is top secret. Only people who know what we're up to are on our side, including the Good Lord. I don't think surprise is going to be an issue." He tapped Mike's knee with the back of his hand. Then, reached into the cargo pocket in his pant leg and produced a folded piece of paper. *"But, just in case, show me what you're talking about."* He said, unfolding the map once pinned to the drawing board in the briefing room where their loadout took place.

Mike spent the next few minutes reviewing the map with his platoon leader. They counseled one another and drew various angles of approach, creating contingencies based on unknown variables. *"Damn, son. Nice job."* Reaper said, as he stood up and began to walk to the front of the truck's massive cargo bed to rap on the rear window and alert the driver of the contingency drop point. He stopped and spun around abruptly to face Mike. *"Do me a favor."*

"Yes sir?" Mike replied.

"Make it through this so I can pin a bar on ya'."

"Yes, sir!"

No sooner had the words left his mouth than a loud boom erupted and shook the entire vehicle. Clamor grew in the cargo bed as the cadre of soldiers reacted. *"Radio contact!"* Reaper barked to the communications officer on board. *"Any wounded?" Once he was satisfied his men were in-tact, he signaled to Mike.*

Shaken, Mike edged forward to the Sergeant who remained collected, as if this was a fly in the kitchen; not an attack on a convoy. "That grenade hit on our left flank. I need you to climb out on the right side and get into the cab with the driver. Guide him straight to your drop point. Looks like they know we're coming!"

"Roger that." Mike said as he rushed past his empty seat. The roads were mostly unpaved, so the M35 was bouncing across the terrain, making it difficult to stand without gripping onto the steel frame that held its canvas cover. Mike slid his hand along the back corner of the steel post, undoing buttons that attached the back canvas panel. Eventually, he made his way down to a kneeling position. He opened it slightly. Lush greenery rushed past as the large truck sped toward its destination. Carefully, he stepped out onto the back bumper and began making his way along the wooden rails leading up to the cab of the truck. Several times, he slipped; but fortunately, recovery was easy with all the places for him to grip onto.

The relief of finally reaching the cab was short-lived. Bullets whizzed past the cab as the convoy began to approach the wooded area flooded with various pockets of KPA soldiers armed with Soviet weaponry. A few metallic thunks sounded as they impacted the driver's side of the truck. Mike knew the M35 could take a serious beating. The trucks would often return to his outpost riddled with bullet holes, but fully functional. He opened the door to the cab and climbed in.

"Glad you made it! You're going to have one wild story to tell!" the driver said to Mike as he settled into the passenger seat.

"Me too!" Mike said. "It's not a good war story if it doesn't start off with being shot at by the bad guys. Hang a right at that clearing between those two trees."

The big truck swung to the right, away from the direction of fire power; placing more trees, brush and cover between the convoy and the bad guys. The world seemed to slow down instantly. The driver was a young crew-cut enlisted officer from Pennsylvania. He looked over at Mike through black-framed Army issue glasses and spread a big grin across his face. "Reaper says you've got a better idea where to dock this land yacht. Let's hear it!"

"Approximately 1.5 clicks ahead, this forest will open up to some rocky terrain with a natural stone barrier to the East. That's our spot." Mike replied. For a moment, he considered the loadout briefing. Based on the position of the original drop point, the men were to exit the deuce-and-a-half on the driver side. The detour they were forced into taking through the brush meant they would arrive from the opposite direction. If their unit disembarked as planned, it would put them directly in the line of fire from the heavy machine gun. He picked up the truck radio to coordinate the exit and the repositioning of the gun-truck. Nothing. "Must have been hit in some of that spray back there. If our guys bail on your side, they're target practice for that KPV and the gun truck won't be able to provide any cover without punching holes through our truck."

"Doesn't look like I'll have time for a 10-point turn to get us facing the right direction, either." The Lieutenant replied. "Private, there's your rock garden." Ahead, a series of large gray stones stood alone in a field of vine covered rock.

"Looked bigger on the map." Mike replied. The unmistakable pop of the 14.5mm KPV machine gun roared in the distance. Rock from the surrounding terrain erupted into a cloud of dust.

"They're on us!" the driver exclaimed as he tugged the wheel to bank the large vehicle closer to the massive stone wall.

"Get there as fast as you can. Then stop as fast as you can!" Mike said as he slung his rifle over his back and strapped on his Army-green domed helmet.

The M35 came to a sliding stop, slamming Mike against the dash, as the KPV continued to reverberate through the trees like some kind of monster playing a cadence. Mike jumped out of the vehicle and ran to the back to alert his unit they were facing the wrong direction. "Passenger side! Passenger side!" he barked over the chaos as he motioned aggressively toward the right side of the truck. He felt two bullets connect as a searing heat began to burn through his leg. An involuntary scream erupted from his lips as the force of the impact dropped him to his knees.

"Gotcha, Private. We've got to get you back to Miss Wyoming!" Reaper's solid frame lifted him with surprising ease and carried him around to the medic who began working on his leg immediately.

The rest of the battle was a blur and Mike was in-and-out of consciousness. But, their support gun-truck was able to maneuver to a good firing position thanks to the rocky outcrop. They disabled the KPV, freeing the communications officer to call in air support. The mission was considered a success.

Later, Mike was awarded his first bar by Sgt. Grimm in a ceremony conducted at the US Army base in Casper, Wyoming. "Miss Wyoming" was in attendance, as were all the soldiers in the unit whose lives Mike saved through his bravery. He was also awarded a Purple Heart and a Bronze Star for his heroism in the line of duty. During his ceremony, Mike humbly expressed to everyone present that it was truly the loadout briefing that earned their success. He was just the messenger.

Preparation is the key to nearly any success. It is lauded as the defining attribute behind everything from acing a test to winning an Olympic medal. In practically any kind of battlefield, it is heralded as the difference between winning and losing. But why is that? What is it about preparation that makes it such a capable predictor of success? And, for our purposes, is there a takeaway for success in sales?

Preparation has multiple positive effects on performance. First, it finds errors before they occur. Second, it creates memory. Third, it frees the mind to focus on other things while tending to the primary duties practiced repeatedly. That's why it gets so much credit for success! Imagine a scenario where you're required to perform, but you are already aware of potential errors, and you know your subject matter so well that you're able to deal with unknown factors while never skipping a beat because you're performing from memory.

Ask a 7-year-old boy what they want to be when they grow up. They will rattle off anything from a professional athlete (insert sport here), to a doctor or a YouTube star. Ask a 7-year-old girl what they want to be when they grow up and you'll get those same answers and then some! Kids dream big! So why is it, then that less than half a percent of the world's population will ever actually play a professional sport? Only half a percent of the world's population will become a practicing physician. And, there are significantly fewer percentage numbers of ballerinas, astronauts, princesses, and people who actually make money on YouTube.

What happens in those years between childhood dreams and adult reality? Preparation.

There are volumes of books written on the subject of what it takes to become a top performer. One thing they all have in common is preparation. In his book, *"Outliers,"* Malcom Gladwell discloses research showing that it takes approximately 10,000 hours of practice to truly become an expert at something. Want to break that down into simpler terms? This means that if you practiced for an hour a day, 365 days a year, it would take about 27 years to be declared a statistical expert. So, let's ask the question again in a different way. What percentage of people in the world are dedicated enough to become experts in their respective fields? Not very many.

The best thing about sales is that there aren't many who actually practice it as a trade craft. It's kind of a bizarre notion, really, considering the attributes of most sales positions. Some or all of your pay is directly related to your ability. Your schedule is typically flexible. And most sales positions also get to enjoy life outside of a cubicle. So, why is it considered by so many to be a contingency plan, rather than a career?

Blame training.

At this point, you shouldn't be surprised by that. If it has been proven that preparation is often a key element in defining success, then our approach to training should change. Today, the average sales rep receives classroom training for 0-3 weeks, endures a 2 month long mentoring/monitoring process and takes nearly a year to become productive (11.2 months). The average tenure of a sales position is less than 2 years. So, really, they're training for a year and producing for a year. It sounds like a wash. Only, it isn't. On average, it costs 1.5 to 2 times a rep's first-year quota to train them. Statistically, more than half of that cost is related to productivity loss during the onboarding process that we just established might be too short!

Imagine that you want to become an Olympic swimmer. You have determined you are the next US Gold Medalist and so you find a coach at the nearby YMCA. That coach teaches you the basics of swimming for 3 weeks. Then, they have you report back to them daily for two months to check in on your progress. You're ready at that point, right?

It sounds ridiculous in those terms, but this is what organizations do to sales people every day. If the organization doesn't treat it like a long-term career, how is the rep supposed to react? Simultaneously, a 27-year-long training would also not be advisable – regardless of how cool Malcom Gladwell may be. So, what do we do? Training is arguably the central issue in today's sales culture. How do we address it?

What if we address the flaws in sales training by addressing the sales method? Perhaps the mantra around the sales profession can become: "You've been preparing for this your entire life!" It certainly beats the current version: "We're going to put you through a few weeks of agonizing hell and then turn you loose. Most of you won't make it past the first 6 months. The rest of you will move on in 2 years. Then, we're going to do this all over again!"

Consultative Sales encourages preparation. There is certainly an element of training involved. You still need to possess basic knowledge of your organization's product or service. But, the process is no longer all about the product; it's about the customer. You've spent your entire life building relationships.

You've celebrated successes. You've endured failures. You're an expert by any standard! And in this role, your primary goal is to know them by consulting with them and resolving their issues with the products and services offered by your organization.

If you think this is an exercise in splitting hairs, it's not. There is a definitive difference in preparing someone to sell a product versus preparing someone to have meaningful conversations and align solutions with needs. Sales training is often the first time a new rep has experienced the nuances and specifications of that particular product or service offering. As a result, half of them won't make it to the statistical two year mark and the other half will make it past it. But every rep in that training class has had a lifetime filled with meaningful conversations. Doesn't it make sense to maximize that experience?

"Wait a minute. Aren't meaningful conversations what Relationship Selling is all about?"

"Yes."

"So you're rebranding Relationship Selling and calling it something else?"

"No."

No one will argue that Relationship Selling is a powerful tool. However, anyone who has practiced it long enough to experience leadership change would also argue that it is a dangerous method. Relationship Selling involves establishing a person-to-person relationship with the decision maker in order to establish trust. This relationship-based trust is what creates value and earns sales.

There are similarities between Relationship Selling and Consultative Sales. Both are established through meaningful conversations. This maximizes the lifelong relationship development experience of the sales professional, placing less emphasis on product knowledge while creating deeper customer relationships.

Relationship Selling creates meaningful dialogue by learning more about the decision maker. Sales professionals skilled at this craft often know names and birth dates of their customer's children and grandchildren. They take clients out to lunches and to play golf. They connect on social media and sometimes even their spouses become socially intertwined! What this style does is essentially create a tightly knit group of friends who only buy from them. Admittedly, they're nearly impossible to sell against. But, this style is also prone to some nasty cause and effect scenarios that can take a secure rep and place them in a very insecure position without notice.

- DECISION MAKER LEAVES : What happens when the person you've spent a decade befriending, leaves? This scenario has burned plenty of Relationship Selling gurus, because they're often replaced by strangers. And that cushy selling relationship you created based on one person is suddenly in total jeopardy. The worst part is, no one else in the company understands your value. Often, you end up having to re-bid your own account, unless the new decision maker also has a friend in the business. Then, you simply lose the account.

- DUNBAR'S NUMBER : British anthropologist, Robin Dunbar, suggested there is a cognitive limit to the number of social connections a person can maintain, based on the size of our neocortex. That number is estimated to be 150. What this means is that your very own brain actually limits your effectiveness in Relationship Selling. And, good sales people don't like being told there are limits.

- TOO CLOSE FOR COMFORT : Relationships are two-way streets. Business ends at a reasonable time each day, but friendship ...well, it is timeless. And that Hallmark-commercial-esque sentence is brought to you by the 8:00pm client call you have to answer because you made them your friend. Face it, sometimes we meet people in business whose company we just can't help but to enjoy. That's different. But if friendship becomes your selling-point then that means you better pick up. You can't be out there looking disingenuous! What will your friends say?

- LONG DISTANCE RELATIONSHIPS ARE HARD : Self-help books on relationships are consistent in one piece of advice: being present. It is difficult to maintain a relationship if you're not actually there. In today's global economy, you may find yourself doing business with a decision maker half way around the world! If being besties is your sales game, that's going to get seriously expensive when you get invited to their Kwanzaa party.

- JEKYLL & HYDE : Buyers have different personality types. How many depends on what your favorite sales book is. Since you're currently reading this one, and this author doesn't particularly subscribe to a one-size-fits-all personality test; we'll say between 4 and 16. Let's say you originally developed a relationship with a #2 personality type. Because you knew them so well, you understood that #2 personalities don't really care about price. They are into customization. So, you sold them a product or service with a really healthy margin that they didn't even consider because your offering could be completely customized by them. But then they retire, only to be replaced by a #4 personality type. Now, #4s are numbers people. They look at what their company has been paying for your product or service over the last decade and are so disgusted, they won't even take your phone calls!

The biggest difference between Consultative Sales and Relationship Selling is that the meaningful relationship you are establishing in Consultative Sales is person-to-organization. The value comes from what you know about their business, rather than what you know about their decision maker. This key difference virtually eliminates every single downside to Relationship Selling; while maintaining the benefits.

So far, we've established that Consultative Sales reduces the training time necessary to become an expert. It increases the number of people capable of becoming an expert. It also creates the potential for long-term employees in a sales force by providing them the benefits of a career in sales, while minimizing stress. The idea of training someone to maximize a skill they've honed for decades mimics a traditional loadout by enabling the sales person to avoid errors, act from memory, and create freedom to handle the unexpected. It also emphasizes the same benefits and deep relationships created by Relationship Selling without the pitfalls.

But, this isn't just about Consultative Sales. It's about you. And you deserve a good shot at this, so here's your loadout. By now, you have a decent grasp for why Consultative Sales makes sense. The rest of this book is designed to provide a framework for you to begin to understand how to implement this powerful sales tool.

- BREAKING BIOLOGY : A Monk and a Tiger illustrate prospecting, from a different point of view.

- CONSCIENTIOUS LEADERSHIP : A sparrow gets her point across to the king of birds , revealing key points on how to establish yourself as the leader without the title.

- ASSESSMENTS : Marie may have lost her glasses, but you'll lose your mind when her story reveals the value of being curious in all the right ways.

- ANALYSIS : A coach with unmotivated players gets the last laugh while driving home a point that resonates with his entire team, inspiring you to leave no stone unturned as you analyze your customers situation using tools taken directly from a consultant's playbook.

- SUMMARY REPORT & PRESENTATION : The values of preparation and performance are emphasized in an historic space flight in a chapter designed to boost your sales into orbit!

All cheesy chapter summaries aside, this book was designed by people like you, to be read by people like you. Every one of our staff members at Handbookguide Business Solutions are sold-out on sales people. We love you. We understand you. We appreciate what you do and what you go through on a daily basis. So, when we sat down to write a book we knew it needed to be short, quasi-entertaining, to the point, and it needed to have pictures. Really awesome pictures. And before you head off on your journey into Consultative Sales, here's your roadmap to the Consultative Sales Cycle:

1. Quantify. Define the quantity of your target market by creating a list of the organizations who fit your ideal customer profile.

2. Qualify. Set initial meetings based on a 7-point touch plan designed to maximize marketing efforts while reducing burnout.

3. Learn. Learn about your qualified prospects in a genuine Q&A designed to uncover pain points and inefficiencies.

4. Assess. Conduct an assessment as a recommended solution to issues uncovered in the "Learn" phase.

5. Analyze. Thoroughly review the assessment in order to identify areas of greatest need and how your organization can impact those through products and services offered.

6. Report. Deliver a detailed summary report to the customer reiterating perceived needs and findings based on analysis conducted; with recommendations for specific products and services offered by your organization.

7. Deliver. Conduct delivery in phases based in order of greatest need.

Chapter 2 : Key Points

- Preparation finds errors before they occur, creates memory, and frees the mind to focus on other things while tending to primary duties
- It takes approximately 10,000 hours of practice to become an expert at something
- Traditional Sales Training is product focused and lasts between 2-3 weeks
- You've spent most of your entire life having meaningful conversations and building relationships
- Avoids pitfalls of Relationship Selling: decision maker leaves, Dunbar's Number, too close for comfort, long-distance relationships, Jekyll & Hyde
- Consultative Sales is not person-to-person, it's person-to-organization
- Sales Cycle:
  - ✓ Quantify
  - ✓ Qualify
  - ✓ Learn
  - ✓ Assess
  - ✓ Analyze
  - ✓ Report
  - ✓ Deliver

Chapter 3

Breaking Biology

No, Walter White does not make an appearance in this chapter. But it does involve science, and as a bonus it will end with a *Breaking Bad* quote!

So, what does biology have to do with consultative sales? It turns out, the answer is: Quite a bit.

As he walked up the stone steps laid centuries ago by monks before him, Chan felt his excitement growing. His dreams as a child connected to years of preparation in his youth and now it was time. He glanced back down the long gray stairway to his family; still waiving at him from hundreds of feet below. Their pride was apparent as they wished their son well.

The moment was cut short when a roar erupted from behind the high stone walls of the monastery. It echoed as it bounced its way around all the hard surfaces of the tall stone mountain. Immediately, the warmth in his heart was replaced by fear. His feet, once lightly carrying him up the daunting pathway were now immovable. He peered into the misty mountain fog before him and saw nothing but the outline of the wall.

With a deep and difficult swallow, he continued ahead. First one step. Then, another. "Was it my imagination?" he wondered.

Another loud roar burst from the interior courtyard of the monastery. This time, there was no mistaking that it was real. It was also closer. Chan began to search his training and his master's teachings for anything that might help him. But there was no recall of anything to deal with this moment. The terror residing in every part of his body begged for him to turn around swiftly and race back down the mountain to the awaiting arms of his family below.

"No." Chan said. "I must go on."

A few more roars arose through the mountain air as he continued his ascent. The size of the walls grew larger. The sounds of the beast grew louder. The monastery was immense. "Any manner of monster could be concealed behind those walls," he thought. His fear grew with everything else. But so did his determination.

Near the only entrance to the monastery, Chan stopped. The high altitude had cleared the fog and he stared at the large arching gateway before him when a familiar voice called out.

"Xiao gunzi!" There was only one person who referred to Chan as "tiny stick."

"Master."

"Your voice quivers." There was a forced curiosity behind the Master's statement. A decade of training had familiarized him with the tactic. This was a test. And whatever was behind that wall was there for him.

"There is something in the courtyard, Master."

"Landscape." The old man responded.

"There is something else."

"Oh! That is old Ya." The Master replied. "He's been here so long he is part of the landscape."

"What is Ya?" Chan questioned while considering that Ya literally means "teeth."

"A tiger." Came the bemused response.

Chan's heart sank to his feet, but the pit of his stomach won the race. He endured years of mental training, meditation and physical conditioning. But nothing had prepared him for this. How was he supposed to face a tiger?

"May I approach him?"

"Why ask now? You've already spent most of your day approaching him." The Master replied, referring to the young monk's long steep climb to the top of the mountain.

Intuitively, Chan knew this was the part of the test where he was supposed to continue moving toward Ya. "Tiny Stick faces giant Teeth," he thought, as his mind replayed images of the slobbery sticks his family dog would often chew on until they broke. "Great. My journey ends as a chew toy."

He cautiously stepped forward beneath the gateway. The courtyard behind the wall was beautiful. Every tree, every stone, and every blade of grass was a carefully manicured collaboration between nature and monk. Its beauty lured him past the entrance. Beyond the picturesque landscape were the large golden doors to the monastery, and for a brief moment he forgot about the hidden danger of the garden.

Ya lept in front of Chan. The creature was stunning. Fire orange fur adorned with patterned black stripes wrapped a girth easily twice that of his own. Two emerald eyes sparkled above a bared set of ivory teeth as if the personification of fear, itself, was crafted by the finest jewler in the land. A massive paw, tipped with black knife-like claws swiped at Chan.

"He does not understand why you are here." The Master called out above the tiger's growls.

Chan opened his mouth to speak his intention, but no words could pass through his tightened throat. Ya advanced toward him and swiped again.

"He also does not speak our language," he said. "Show him who you are without speaking."

"You did not train me for this!" Chan replied, angrily, allowing the intensity of the moment to get the better of him.

"I didn't know I had to." Came the indignant reply. "You mean you don't know how not to be scary?"

As if cued by the word scary, Ya charged Chan. He stopped just a few feet away and swiped at him again. His claws missing the young monk's customary crimson robe by inches.

"I'm not the one who is scary!" screamed Chan.

"Not accordingto him." The Master replied.

Chan considered for a moment the viewpoint of the beast. He was a stranger. And, although he would reside here for the remainder of his life, this was the tiger's home. He had not done anything to prove to the tiger that he had no intention to hurt him. Instead, Chan just wandered inside the garden, drawn in by its beauty, and made no consideration for its resident.

Chan slowly backed away until he was outside the courtyard. Ya began to calm, and although his teeth were still bared, the growling and swiping had stopped. Chan grabbed the sleeve of his crimson robe and tore it off. He placed it just beneath the large gateway. Then, he knelt down and waited. For over an hour he watched as Ya would slowly approach the sleeve and its former owner and then bounce away from it quickly. With each approach, the tiger seemed more confident.

Finally, the tiger sniffed the sleeve before pawing at it and carrying it in its mouth to a spot beneath a nearby tree. Chan used the opportunity to reach his sleeveless arm across the threshold into the courtyard. He held it there, palm open, before peering around the wall to the spot where Ya was staring back at him. The torn red sleeve rested beneath one giant paw.

Saying nothing, Chan continued calmly and slowly into the courtyard. His hands were open, and his eyes rested on the tiger as he remarked at the wonder of such a creature. Chan remained calm. Pleasant. And as he passed the tiger, Chan kept his body turned toward him so that Ya would always be comforted by where his focus remained. As he made his way across the great garden to the golden doors, the tiger would occasionally even appear to lose interest in him; preferring, instead, to paw at the discarded sleeve.

Once he had reached the entrance to the monastery, the tall golden door opened. There stood his Master, smiling. Chan fell through the opening and slumped to the floor. A combination of exhaustion and relief overcame him.

"It is a small price to pay to give of yourself to ensure the comfort of a stranger," he said. "Come. You need a new robe."

Much like "Ya" in the story above, every person you meet is programmed by instinct. It's inherent in our DNA. It's biological. It's animalistic. And you can't uninstall the program. But you can recognize it and work with it.

Thousands of volumes on sales focus on how to properly conduct yourself in an appointment or how to close a sale. But, what good does any of that do for you if you're unsure as to how to get there in the first place? For a moment, consider that you are like Chan. You've spent time being groomed for the position you now find yourself in. This is your moment to shine. So, with all the determination and intent you can carry, you begin your approach.

Remember that one of the key elements to Consultative Sales is the idea that anyone in your target market can eventually become a customer. This means your goal is not to expend the tremendous effort it takes to go from mountain top to mountain top looking for the monastery without a tiger in its courtyard. It's not a numbers game. It is a game of understanding the tiger.

Decision makers are hounded by sales people playing the numbers game. The marketers call because the organization is on their list and the decision maker is named. When the decision maker deflects the call, one of two abusive outcomes occurs:

One: They don't call again.

Two: They call incessantly.

This practice is one of the things that has given a negative connotation to sales. The decision maker is either left to feel unimportant or harassed. Because of these (frankly) abusive practices, decision makers are naturally untrusting of new vendor relationships. It creates the same kind of wary attention between you and your potential customers that Ya gave to Chan upon their first interaction. They don't know you're not scary. So, you need to take the time to show them why you are there.

That makes your initial contact about Quality over Quantity. After all, "time" plays a key role in the quality of something. Let's use shoes as an example. At some point, you have likely had an experience in making the decision to purchase a cheap pair of shoes. Economics 101 tells us that the reason some shoes are $20 and other shoes with similar colors are $200 is due to production volume. Company "A" pumps out 1,000 shoes a day using a production line that is mostly automated and geared toward discount-store volume. Their shoes retail for $20. Company "B" makes only 100 shoes a day, but each shoe is hand-sewn by artisans who take pride in their craft and leave a signed quality notecard in each shoebox. Their shoes retail for $200.

If you were given a budget of $200 for shoes, would you go buy 10 pairs of the mass-produced Company "A" shoe? Or would you purchase one pair of hand-crafted Company "B" shoe?

Most of you will choose the $200 shoe. (Some of you are still trying to figure out a way to purchase one $20 pair and pocket the change. Please give up sales, immediately, and go work in government accounting. They truly need you!)

Those of you who chose the $200 shoe have likely had an experience with a "cheap" shoe. It wasn't a good one. So, the thought of 10 pairs of a bad thing sounds even worse than 1 pair of them! Quantity is not favorable in this example.

Consider the words used to describe the $200 shoe: *"Hand-sewn by artisans who take pride in their craft and leave a signed quality notecard in each shoebox."* Hand-sewn implies that the interaction is one-on-one. Your shoe is being made by a person, not a machine. Artisan implies that they are not working in a cavernous, dimly lit dungeon in a low-wage country. Your shoe is made by a person who considers shoes art. Craft implies this company does not have a revolving-door in their HR department. Your shoe is made by someone with time-tempered skill and experience in shoe-making. And the fact that they leave a signed notecard in each shoebox makes it personal. Your shoe is made by someone who takes enough pride in the shoe that they literally put their name on it.

Imagine taking that same approach to sales. Do you think today's buyer is looking for someone who treats them like a $20 shoe, or a $200 shoe?

Today's buyer is searching for quality. And most of them don't know where to go to find it. Did you know that a study conducted in 2018 showed that 82% of buyers felt sales people were unprepared for sales?

Taking the qualities of the artisan shoemaker, how do you think those buyers would feel about sales people if their interactions were:

- Personal / One-on-one
- With someone who considers selling an "art"
- Who has time-tempered skill and experience in meaningful conversation
- Who takes pride in their work and ensures every step in the process has their signature on it

Undoubtedly, showcasing the attributes of an artisan shoemaker would reveal the quality of the sales person – and therefore the sale – to the buyer.

Time is a factor in quality. So, how much time does it take to show quality to a potential customer?

Statistically, it takes 7 quality touches to convert a prospect to a customer. The word "quality" indicates that those touches should not all be by phone and they should also not all occur within the same week (or day – don't be that person). A "touch" is defined as a *quality* contact. That "quality" part is vital. It should be a contact where effort is put forth to show the customer that you understand them and that you are not out to get them.

Sales is a follow-up game.

To keep you on your follow-up game, consider creating a 7-point Touch Plan. This enables you to keep your focus on quality, rather than quantity. It also keeps the pressure off both parties (you and the buyer) by not assuming a sale is expected in the first contact. Instead, it is the beginning of a fact-finding exercise geared toward trust and relationship building. The initial call is now exactly that: an initial call. You've statistically got 6 more meaningful points of contact before the magic starts to happen, and it will. Below is a list of 7 sample quality touches.

1. **Introductory Call** – Resist the temptation to make this call about you. It's not. You're calling as a consultant. You are calling to learn more about them. It makes the call easier, you naturally sound like less of a robot, and it prevents you from trying to squeeze in every fact you were trained on about your organization.

2. **Handwritten Thank You** – If your handwriting stinks, find someone to write it for you. It is that important. These go a long way, so don't take the easy way out. An email just doesn't convey the same level of quality. Hand-write your thank you note.

3. **Send Item of Interest** – This can be virtually anything related to their interests, as long as it's not

about you. Maybe you learned they have a hobby and you found a cool article about it. Maybe there is some brand-new ground-breaking research on THEIR industry. Maybe it's a follow-up to a question they asked in a previous conversation. Regardless, make sure you are acutely aware of whose interest you're pacifying, here.

4. **Follow up Call** – Follow up on the item you sent. This is a simple, hey I just wanted to see if you got it. What did you think about it? Ask them if it changed anything relative to the Item of Interest. Did you guys book a vacation there, yet? Did you show the article to your sales team? Have you tried out that golf club yet?

5. **Invite to Learn More** – Notice that so far, you've not really done much to "push" your products and services. This is the time where you get to invite them to learn more about your products and services. Think of a webinar, an open house or a lunch & learn opportunity. Even though you are inviting them to know more about you, it STILL needs to be about them. Base your invite around their situation.

6. **Send Bullet Point Reminder** – Maybe they accepted your invite. Maybe they didn't. Maybe they said they would come and didn't show. Or, maybe they attended and even brought some others from their organization. It doesn't matter. Any of those outcomes is a great reason to send out a brief reminder of the key takeaways from the event. Remember, if they showed up, send it with a handwritten thank you!

7. **Ask for the Next Level** – At this point, you've done all the right things. Because you've kept the focus on them, you now know more about them than you did when you started. You might have some idea of their issues (as either an organization, or as an industry as a whole) or why an assessment could be beneficial to them. At the very least, you will be able to put things into a perspective that is personal to them.

In the story of the young monk, Chan had to exercise patience while he waited for the tiger to realize he was not a threat. The tiger approached the sleeve repeatedly before gaining the confidence to pick it up. The confidence the tiger was testing was not its own. It's a tiger. It clearly displayed its confidence while operating as though Chan was a threat. The purpose for the multiple approaches was to help the tiger gain confidence in Chan. Taking the time to create 7 quality touches with a potential customer works in the same way. It is a method to help them gain confidence in you.

Similarly, you might feel that approaching an unknown decision maker is somewhat scary. But, once you see a "sales person" from their viewpoint, you might just realize that you are actually the scary one in the scenario and trust must be established in order to move forward. The good news is that trust is negotiable. As Walter White once said, "Name one thing in this world that is not negotiable."

Chapter 3 : Key Points

- We are biologically wired to mistrust the unfamiliar.
- If you think the decision maker is scary, you should see the way you appear to them.
- Set the tone by keeping your focus on the customer.
- It is a small price to pay to give of yourself to ensure the comfort of a stranger.
- Today's buyer is looking for Quality over Quantity.
- Take on the attributes of the artisan shoemaker by keeping your interactions personal, meaningful, experienced, and with your signature on quality.
- It statistically takes 7 "quality touches" to convert a prospect to a customer.
- Create a 7-point Touch Plan to track your progress with each potential customer.
- When you are ready to take it to the "next level," understanding of the needs of customer and the decision maker goes a long way.
- The good news is that trust is negotiable.

Chapter 4

Conscientious Leadership

One of the key qualities of a good marketer is leadership. But, the world of information is confusing when it comes to leadership. Depending upon who you ask, there are anywhere between 4 to 12 different leadership styles. Some sound delightful. Some sound a bit tyrannical. And others sound barely like leadership at all. Vince Lombardi is quoted to have said that

"Leaders are made, not born." Meanwhile, the Great Man theory and Trait theories believe that certain genetic qualities make people better suited for leadership.

The great thing is that Conscientious Leadership is simple. It is something anyone can learn. And it is the kind of leadership required for Consultative Selling.

She felt confident as she watched the sun peek over the trees along the Eastern side of the forest. Sparrow was exhausted but pleased with her work. All night long she had labored in the Great Tree, twisting and twining small branches together to resemble a loosely woven basket. She flew up near the top of the tree, where Crow oversaw the birds of the forest, to hear his morning address.

Again, the birds of the forest complained of the growing gnat population.

"I understand, but there simply are not enough small birds to control the population," said the wise old bird. Crow was a regal animal, especially in the sunlight where his feathers reflected colors in hues of purple, blue and gold. He was easily twice as large as the nearest bird and his piercing eyes and large black beak gave an ominous compliment to his majesty. Crow's voice echoed through the forest when he spoke. "It will die

down in the cooler weather as it always does. In the meantime, continue to rub your feathers in the pines of the Northern Forest to keep them at bay."

"I'm going to build a new nest in this tree." Sparrow said to Crow.

He calmly informed her, "That would be a mistake. The current nesting arrangement is just fine."

"I'm GOING to build a new nest in this tree," she replied. The dappled sunlight broke through the trees just above her head, adding to the notion that the whole forest was watching her every move.

The other birds of the forest grew concerned. No one had ever moved their nest before. Besides that, no one had certainly ever confronted Crow like this.

"You see, it's actually not fine at all. No bird here enjoys viewing your morning address through a fog of insects. No bird here is fond of the feeling of a biting gnat between their feathers. The pine works for a few hours until it wears off. A more permanent solution would be to increase the number of small birds, and to no longer isolate them to the East in order to better control the gnat population." Sparrow continued. "My nest is small. And it only holds 2 chicks. It would help with the gnats if sparrows were to have 3 or perhaps even 4 chicks and to hatch *them on this side of the forest. So, I'm simply going to build a new nest in this tree."*

Crow sighed as he tilted his towering head down to gaze at the tiny bird. *"It is widely regarded that I'm the wisest bird in the forest. And I am informing you that this experiment of yours will only end in tragedy,"* he boomed. *"You see, this tree is on the West side of the forest. And everyone knows that the wind storms blow in from the West side. Only the biggest and strongest birds who build the biggest and strongest nests can build their nests here.*

"Your nest is tiny so that it is not easily seen by Hawk, since you cannot protect yourself. Your nest holds 2 eggs because Sparrows should hatch no more than 2 at a time. Your nest is also on the East side of the forest so that all the trees of the forest have a chance to buffer the wind as it blows in from the West. So, it would be a mistake for you to change."

At the sound of this declaration, the birds began chirping and flapping. *"Indeed, this is why Crow is considered to be so wise,"* said Finch.

Expecting the debate was over, Crow hoisted his great shimmering wings when Sparrow again interrupted. *"The only reason we have 2 is because the nest is too small for any more."* She said. *"And there is a reason you believe wind storms only* come from the West. *The storms arriving from the East do not affect the West because of the same grove of trees you think buffer the East. Also, Hawk leaves us alone. She knows she cannot win a race with me through the branches. Nor could any other bird her size!"*

A hush fell over the forest. No one was chirping. No one was even moving. But Sparrow, with the light still beaming across her golden head, tilted it to gaze back up at the great wise bird and waited for him to speak. Seconds were made minutes in the still silence. Sparrow wanted to burst, but preparation for this moment kept her calm.

"You mean my size?" Crow asked.

"Yes." Sparrow replied, keeping her gaze locked on his. "Even you, Crow."

Cawing laughter grew from his beak as it rang through the trees. "Oh Sparrow. Surely you know that you would not stand a chance in a race through the trees with a bird like me."

"Not just any tree." She stated. "This one."

"This one?" He asked, sounding surprised. "My tree. The Great Tree?"

She stood firm in her resolve, nodding once in agreement.

Suddenly, Crow saw a way to save Sparrow from herself and to re-establish himself as the one true, wise leader of the forest.

"Why don't we see?" he asked. "You can lead and I will pursue. But when I pluck one feather from your tail, you must abandon this nonsense about changing the nesting arrangement."

"And when I win?" she asked.

"Ha!" the great bird chuckled. "IF you win, you can build your nest here."

"When I win, I won't have to," she stated, and immediately leapt into flight.

Crow sprang from his perch and extended his wings with a sound like the rushing wind. He could see her below, darting through clumps of leaves. His beak thrust forward as he tightened his wings against his back and began to dive toward her. To the forest birds watching, he was a blur. But to him, things seemed to move more slowly as he took in the small bird's trajectory and aligned with it.

Crow cast a shadow when he leapt from the tree. She could feel the sun disappear behind him. In no time at all, his streamlined profile had carried him right to her. She rolled a wing beneath her and flipped to the side, narrowly escaping between two clumps of leaves. Shapes of green confetti followed her as his massive beak broke through the leaves effortlessly. Behind her, she could see them falling.

"Good." She thought as she clipped into an upward climb with rapid beats of her compact wings.

"Close," said Crow, noting the sweet taste of the leaves still on his tongue. "Next time."

Above him, a tiny shape zoomed out of the tree. "There is no way," he thought, trying to calculate the speed of her ascent. She swiftly inverted and dove toward him, before darting into the tree again just feet above his head.

With no room for him to turn, he thrashed his wings to climb to her position. The small branches and leaves were no match for his mighty wings and crumbled below him, creating a contrail of tree parts in his wake. Through the onslaught of leaves and limbs brushing across his face, he searched for her. But her size and color made her practically invisible in the Great Tree's lush foliage.

"Crow!" she shouted as she swept past his head before diving again.

Frustrated by the futile chase, he opened his beak and snapped at everything near him as he heaved his great body into the space away from the tree before locating her dive and matching it to his own. Glints of blues and purple shimmered off his majestic feathers as he turned away from the sun and dove toward her. As if threading a needle, she moved effortlessly through the small gaps created by spaces between the dense green canopy. His size didn't allow him the luxury of dodging anything. He aimed his great beak toward the last place he saw her and tumbled through a cacophony of leaves, twigs and stems. His vision was blurred by the thrashing foliage around him. With his sight rendered useless, Crow closed his eyes and listened for her. He could only hear the percussion of every impact. He tried to taste the air, but the sweet earthy leaves were all that remained on his tongue.

Suddenly, his head impacted a soft cradle that stopped his flailing descent. Unsure of what had happened, he opened his eyes. As his eyes came into focus, he saw the sky through the branches above him. He had landed on his back. Dancing through the sky, falling gently toward him were more shreds of leaves. He could see his path clearly in the damage left behind. Curious as to what softened his fall, he flipped around quickly and rose to his feet.

"Crow." Sparrow's soft voice whispered. "Thank you."

He cast her a puzzled glance. Then, he noticed the delicately woven branches; clearly the work of a small bird. He looked around at his feet to see the bed of fallen leaves he had created in his pursuit of her. In that moment, the clarity of Sparrow's genius became real to him. In blindly chasing after

Sparrow, he had actually helped to create what he was trying to prevent. And in her loving wisdom, she had used her creation to save him from himself.

"*Sparrow.*" *He said.* "*Thank you.*"

- **Conscientious.** Miriam-Webster defines it as meticulous or careful. Its root is found in the term conscience which means to know.

- **Leadership.** Miriam-Webster defines it as the act or office of a leader. Its root is found in the term leader which is a derivative of an old English term, "laeden," meaning "to go."

If you were to take everything you just learned about those two words and combine it into a sentence, it might sound something like this:

> "*Conscientious Leadership is the meticulous act*
> *of a leader who knows where they are going.*"

Few of today's leaders could be described as meticulous or careful. But perhaps even fewer seem to "know where they are going." Conscientious Leadership is a unique brand of leadership comprised of the characteristics that make Sparrow so effective in her story. Its such an uncommon form of leadership that there's a good chance you judged Crow was the leader at first. He was all the things we expect from a Leader. He was powerful. He held an office of leadership. He was unwavering. In a sense, he was even kind as he hoped only to protect Sparrow from making a decision he believed she would regret. And everyone knows Crows are loud.

Contrast that with Sparrow. She was small and quiet. She held no power. She did not hold any office. And to make her odds even more unfavorable, Sparrow came from another part of the forest. She was also in pursuit of a change to the status quo, and, organizations are generally not fond of change.

From a distance, we all love the Sparrow. We celebrate her fighting spirit, but few of us would take the next step and sign up to join her. Something in our human nature creates this deep-seated belief that we are supposed to follow the Crows.

In Consultative Selling, you are often put into the position of the Sparrow. And you are most effective when you are dealing directly with the Crow. Because of the challenges that scenario presents, it is vital to practice Conscientious Leadership during every interaction with the decision maker.

Here are the 5 Acts of Conscientious Leadership:

Act 1: Begin with the End in Mind

Author Stephen R. Covey listed this Act as the second habit in his book, "7 Habits of Highly Successful People." He believed that most people worked hard but noted few successfully got very far. In his book, he attributes their lack of progress to a lack of vision. There should be a goal or a plan in your mind before you simply "go" or "lead."

In the first line of the story, Sparrow completed the framework required to achieve her goal. Her vision was to build a nest in the Great Tree. She knew Crow's strengths and weaknesses. She thought ahead, to him wanting to save her from herself. Rather than thwarting his leadership, she used it. But she also knew that she, too, would have to lead for everyone to see her vision. By the end of the story, Crow realized it was Sparrow leading the entire time.

Did you ever watch a great mystery where the defense attorney asks all the right questions and suddenly the witness, not the defendant, becomes the guilty party? To do their job correctly the attorney had to start at the end and work backward; delicately weaving the questions together in a way that made sense. Similarly, you should set a goal for each interaction with a customer. Then, plan out how you intend to achieve it. Anticipate alternative scenarios. Anticipate failing. Anticipate objections. In any interaction, you should be thinking several steps ahead of the current question. As a Consultant, it is often your job to lead others where they never intended to go, or where they would not have gone without your involvement. That is what establishes your value as a leader and as a consultant.

Act 2: Set the Stage

People often ask what the number one key to Conscientious Leadership is. While it takes all 5 Acts to truly encompass the concept; Setting the Stage is the most vital. So, what does it mean to Set the Stage? Communication.

At the beginning of every appointment, set the stage that you are leading the meeting and they are free to sit back and follow along. That's right. They are free to follow along. Decision makers are accustomed to quarterbacking nearly every aspect of their lives. They constantly manage – at the work place and in their home. Most even end up managing in their volunteer work as an appointed or elected board member! What a relief it is to let them know that you've got this and they can sit back and follow along. You are not taking anything away from them in their decision-making capacity. But, you will accept ownership of this particular interaction and it is one less thing for them to manage. In time, by owning each interaction, they will come to view you as an equal, and eventually rely upon your advice. That is a non-negotiable component to a successful consultative relationship.

You can own a meeting by starting before it even begins. When you greet the decision-maker use their name first. Use their name first. I repeat, use their name first. This is a race, and you have to delicately win. As they are approaching you, wait for the comfortable distance (you will know it by feel); say their name. Or, if you are being escorted to their office or conference room, say it the moment you round the corner and they make eye contact. "Hi, Shelley!" Then, once you've said theirs, you can introduce yourself. "I'm Pennie with Consultation Creation!"

Introductions are a breeze, but it's the next part where people get hung up and run into that empty dead space where great beginnings go to die! Now what? The introduction has happened. Who speaks next? What do they say? This awkward interplay is a joy to watch at networking events if you are a fan of people watching. It's a moment of excruciating, mind-bending silence as both search for something to say and then ..."How are you?"

Never do that.

"How are you?" should be eradicated from the socially acceptable human interaction dictionary, if there is such a thing. It is the most interesting socially acceptable "pass" you will find in conversation, outside of the $100,000 Pyramid game show. It is quite literally a formality. That's all. One person asks and the other replies with a general nondescript affirmative like "fine" or "good." To answer the question with any real meaning is a faux pas. Then the replier returns the favor, lobbing the conversation ball back over the net, "How are you?" The original requestor then replies with another general nondescript affirmative. What's mind-blowing is that you can also watch people do this at hospitals and funerals. "How are you?" Really? At a hospital? At a funeral? "Fine."

Instead, fill the space with what is referred to as a situational condition. First, this allows you the opportunity to speak first. It differentiates you from all the unprofessional people who ask how they are. It also begins to cue the decision maker into the fact that you are capable of leading the conversation. A situational condition contains both things; a condition and a situation.

You can literally play the match game across both columns.

Condition	Situation
• I'm so happy	• We finally connected
• It is an honor	• You took the time to see me
• It is exciting	• To learn more about your organization

There are literally endless situational conditions you can come up with. Just make certain the events leading up to the appointment fit the situation, and the condition fits the personality of the decision maker. In other words, don't tell a Type A CEO of a large Accounting Firm that you are so happy to see them. Likewise, don't tell the rare decision maker who accepts your appointment in your first phone call that you "finally connected."

So, now, the introduction we are building sounds a bit like this:

"Hi Shelly! I'm Pennie with Consultation Creation. It is an honor to be here. Thank you for taking the time to see me."

Often, they will respond to this type of introduction. Read it in their facial expression or body language. If you see a response coming, stop and let them respond. Next, reaffirm the appointment time. This step is simple, but vital to confirm you are leading the appointment. "The calendar invite sent to you scheduled our meeting to run 15 minutes. Does that still work for you?" No matter what, you must allow a response to this. Most often, the response will be confirmation. If not, be gracious but firm. Remember, it is all about the customer.

Communication, or Setting the Stage, is key in every meeting. Not just the first. In subsequent meetings, always begin by bringing them back to why you are meeting. There is a specific 3 step process for a brief recap to keep it short, meaningful, and customer-centric.

1. In our last meeting, you...
2. As a result, my team...
3. Today, we are...

By leading the communication, you become the architect of the dialogue. It allows you to "Set the Stage" every time you interact with the customer. Leadership becomes a byproduct, rather than the goal.

Act 3: Use Command Expression

As a consultant, whose job it is to be the most curious person in the room, you will ask a lot of questions. The catch is to keep it lively and balanced so that it doesn't become an interrogation. Command Expression also allows you to establish leadership and break up an endless stream of questions by commanding an answer, rather than asking for one.

Sounds kind of harsh, right? But that's what it is. Commanding an answer. Clearly, inflection plays a key role when utilizing this tool. And when used correctly, it is an incredible way to continue your quest for knowledge while also diligently earning your leadership status.

EXAMPLES OF COMMAND EXPRESSION

Instead of:

"How does your organization make buying decisions?"

Say:

"Tell me about your purchasing process."

Instead of:

"Do you guys get audited?"

Say:

"Describe the different audit schedules your organization has."

Instead of:

"Does your sales force submit orders from the field?"

Say:

"Explain how an order is started from the field."

Act 4: Honesty at Any Price

You just completed an assessment and have a growing list of recommendations before even doing one bit of analysis. The President of the organization approaches you and says, "So, now that you've seen our organization, tell me what you think." It is the consultative equivalent to being asked how someone looks in an outfit they last wore over a decade ago. (The right answer to the outfit question, by the way, is to enthusiastically ask them how it makes them feel. Answer the question with a question. That is a consultant mindset!) Interestingly, the tactic is also helpful when addressing the President's question.

"I've got a bit of analysis to do before I start forming my own opinions. But your insight is valuable! Tell me what you Feel about your organization."

Think and Feel are two diametrically opposed functions. If you ask someone what they think, they generally rattle it off quickly. If you ask someone what they feel, they often pause or look up before answering (a sign of introspection).

A Conscientious Leader is meticulous and careful. They care too greatly about the result to muddy up the middle. There are tactful ways to express negative information or a differing opinion, and one of those is to use the customer's own insight. If you're meeting and they know you're a consultant, then they already know their organization isn't perfect. Draw out this valuable information by asking what they Feel about their own organization. Or, you can deploy conflicting logic.

Conflicting logic is a dynamic tool in selling. By definition, it is a statement whose logic conflicts with a previous statement or belief. Sparrow used conflicting logic to openly communicate to Crow that he had old or inaccurate information about which direction wind storms come through the forest. In the story, she was a bit short and that is certainly a tool you can hold onto (there are times where it works well). But, there is a softer way to apply conflicting logic to convey honest opinions. Referring to the example question used above, we can assume the President is (rightfully) in love with his organization. A response using conflicting logic might sound something like this:

"It is very clear that you have a lot of potential in your organization. You can be proud of that! But, I'm also excited that you decided to move forward with an assessment because it will be an honor to work together to improve it. And, it is my goal that you will also be proud of that!"

Under no circumstances should you ever try to avoid delivery of negative information in a consultative sale. First, it is disingenuous to the customer. Second, if you falsely deliver that there are no issues, then there are also no solutions. You just wasted everyone's time. And always remember, if someone takes a meeting with a consultant, they already know their organization can improve.

Act 5: Calm Confidence

It's not always easy to remain calm in the world of sales. Customers can throw some pretty surprising things your way. Sometimes, one stray phone call with your organization's back office can unexpectedly destroy a sale; upending months or even years of work. But here's a dynamic shift for your sales thought process: you owe it to your customer not to give up.

Recall that Consultative Sales is truly about uncovering need, and then presenting a phased approach to resolution through your organization's marketable output. If there is need, then there is also "pain" associated with that need.

In the story above, there was a pest issue. Crow's solution was merely one of abatement. The birds of the forest were experiencing a pain associated with need. Their leader did not have all the information necessary to solve their problem. So, he tried adjusting their expectations. A pest-free life was impossible, so brushing against pine needles helped to keep the pests away. It wasn't perfect. But it was something. Sparrow knew the solution. But, she didn't merely approach Crow with a suggestion. She re-established the pain their group was experiencing, settled in with it, and then held it there for all to see. Once she had done that, she moved onto points of conflicting logic. And, she did it in front of an audience of her peers while confronting a much larger bird.

Sparrow exudes Calm Confidence.

Have you ever heard the saying that "sales are made in the void of voices?" It is perhaps the truest and most universal statement about sales. Silence is golden. And it is also a tool that can be used to help you to display Calm Confidence.

In any interaction with a customer, moments of silence tend to feel awkward. If you aren't careful, it can cause your brain to scramble for a sentence to eradicate the uncomfortable moment. This is where mistakes get made. It is where even seasoned and experienced reps oversell, offer unnecessary discounts, or include an "oh by the way" that rarely adds any value. What's interesting is those tactics tend to decrease the confidence of the decision maker. It works against you, and therefore against the customer.

You can't relieve their need-based pain if you can't help them agree on a solution. Learn to enjoy the silence.

Try shifting the focus away from what you are feeling during a pause in conversation to examine the decision maker. What is their body language? What is their face saying? Are they subconsciously nodding their head in agreement? Do they look puzzled? Most often, moments of silence can actually give way to moments of clarity, followed by a reveal.

Silence isn't the only time where Calm Confidence is your ally. One of the worst habits sales reps can develop is overtalk. In a sense, sales professionals quite literally live and die by their words. The traditional sales model teaches that if you say the right things, you get the sale. Mess up, and you lose a commission. It creates an irrational dependence upon vocalization. It also projects a belief that your words are your most valuable asset.

Pitfalls to overtalk can include everything from interrupting a customer while they are talking (this happens all the time) to not allowing the customer to get a word in edgewise. Both are detrimental to sales. Plus, the customer is made to feel "sold to" rather than "understood." Which would you rather feel? Yeah. So would the customer.

Occasionally, the customer misunderstands something you said. The knee-jerk, overtalk reaction is to jump in there and correct them. Immediately. So, the rep – believing they live and die by their own words – interrupts the decision maker. Once your words become more important than the customer's, you lose.

Instead, try the finger-tap method. Any time a customer says something that is either incorrect or reveals another talking point for you, place a finger on a solid surface. Use the arm of a chair or the edge of a table. Each time you feel prompted to speak, place another finger. Then, once they are finished speaking, work your way back through each of the fingers you placed down to either correct their understanding or reveal your talking point. If you forget, then the chances are it wasn't a valuable point to make. Move onto the next.

In Consultative Selling, the customers words are your most valuable asset. Your livelihood depends upon your ability to ask questions, not to make statements. Your ability to sit comfortably in the silence establishes your confidence and reaffirms you are a professional. And, your ability to use silence as a tool, confirms your role as a conscientious leader.

Chapter Four : Key Points

- Conscientious Leadership is the meticulous act of a leader who knows where they are going
- It is the most effective form of leadership in a Sales Person's role because you are often tasked with "leading from behind"
- 5 Acts of Conscientious Leadership
  - o Begin with the end in mind
  - o Set the Stage
  - o Use Command Expression
  - o Honesty at Any Price
  - o Calm Confidence

Chapter 5

Assessment

Performing a true assessment provides you with a huge advantage. Traditional Sales takes a bit of a scattered approach to finding a customer's needs scenario. It's craps-table sales and it puts you and the customer at a distinct disadvantage. A proper assessment allows you to gather detailed information about the customer before presenting any type of solution to the decision maker. It allows for input from other parties and other departments. Assessments present unique and tangible benefits to the organization. They also more than double your chances of closing more than one product line with the customer.

Marie groaned. She loathed the sound of her alarm clock. It wasn't so bad when the sound was coming from Ed's side of the bed. She missed him. Not one to dwell on such things, her withered hand stretched over to the nightstand where well-manicured fingers seemed to dance about before finding the off switch.

"Finally." She breathed a sigh of relief.

Her eyes glanced at the clock. 6:30. A glint of morning light caught her eye as it reflected off the picture frame next to the clock. It was her and Ed at their daughter's wedding. She remarked at the lines on his face, grateful for the 52 years of laughter that put them there. She noted the way the texture of his storm-gray wavy hair complimented the blue suit he wore that day. He was a handsome man.

"Oh my glasses." She sat up, now perched on the edge of her bed. "Marie, you silly girl. You've misplaced them again!"

Most nights, Marie put her glasses beneath that picture. But, lately, she's been staying up late doing crosswords at the kitchen table from a book she was gifted by a friend at her water aerobics class. "It has completely thrown me off my glasses game," she laughed.

In her matching robe and slippers, Marie made her way to the kitchen. She reached into the cupboard for her coffee can. Decaf. "Oh no sir, Mister Juan Valdez. It will be full-strength for me this early in the morning," she said, gently lifting the can from its shelf high above her head. As she scooped the coffee into the filter, she made a quick glance around the counter top for her glasses. "Now where could they be?" she wondered. She cast a glance at the clock on the oven across the kitchen. 6:51. "I'd better get a move on if I'm going to find them in time to leave here by 7:20!"

From the time she was a child, she loved puffed rice cereal. Marie preferred the unsweetened kind so that she could add 2 spoonfuls of sugar to it. There was just something to that crunchy milk at the bottom of the bowl. She poured the cereal into her white porcelain bowl, dreaming about the taste. A few small grains of puffed rice seemed to hop out of the bowl and land on her wooden floors. She glanced down, spotting the tiny specks near her feet. It was amusing to her the way the grains of cereal blended so well with the floor.

She grabbed the milk with her bowl and made her way to the small table in the corner of the kitchen. On the table was the folded book, opened to the crossword she worked last night. A quick glance over to the remaining word took her mind back to the night before. She stopped for a moment to read it. "Seven letter word ending in 't;' synonym for advise."

She pondered the clue for a bit when she was interrupted by Bigs, her tabby cat, as he leapt onto the table top and stood in front of her. She reached out to pet him as she continued to spoon cereal into her mouth. His pink collar jingled as her hand passed over it. Marie examined the purple ID tag dangling from the collar, noting that it had been worn by time, scratching, and general kitty naughtiness. The last digit in her etched phone number was barely recognizable. "Your little tag is looking worn, Bigsie! Don't go running off this afternoon or no one will be able to reach me to come rescue you. And no one but me would put up with you, Mister."

Bigs always seemed to understand when she was picking on him. Maybe it was the inflection in her voice. The cat gave her a displeased groan and flicked his tail in a serpentine fashion.

"Grumpy." She accused. "Speaking of grumpy, I've got to find those glasses or I'll be late to the Hair Salon and Mittie will tar-and-feather me!"

Bigs cocked his head, stared at her and uttered a slight meow.

"Oh really, big boy?" She asked. "You run off with 'em?"

Marie picked up after her breakfast and put the milk in its place on her way out of the kitchen. As she closed the refrigerator door, she chuckled at a Maxine card hung by a magnet. It was a gift from her long-time friend and stylist, Mittie, this year on her birthday. The sour old Maxine character stood there, drink in hand, and ballcap backwards with a caption in small print that read: "Age doesn't make you forgetful. Having way too many stupid things to remember makes you forgetful."

"Ha! How true!" Marie said, tapping the card with her finger. "Especially this morning! Where are my glasses?"

Marie rounded the corner to her bedroom, grabbed the dress she always word on her hair days, and made her way to the sink to brush her teeth. She slid open the drawer containing the various ointments, pastes and creams she's collected over the years. "Better make sure not to use the hemorrhoid cream again, old girl," she muttered to herself, as she recalled the awful texture it left in her mouth for hours after mistaking the tube for toothpaste. Looking down, Marie read the label on the special medicated toothpaste her dentist had prescribed.

Beneath it, in small print, was the active ingredient "1.1% Potassium Chloride," she read aloud. "No clue what it is, but it beats whatever's in the butt cream!"

She gently squeezed the toothpaste across her brush. She turned on the faucet to lightly wet the bristles and then looked up into the mirror in front of her for the first time that day. Her eyes grew wide, her mouth gaped, and then she began to chuckle. The chuckle grew into laughter as she leaned over the sink and looked closer into the mirror.

"My glasses!" she exclaimed.

Often, an organization's leadership team experiences difficulty identifying a problem because they are looking "through" the problem. It has become their way of work, and therefore they can't see around it. In the story, Marie can't find her glasses because she is literally looking through them! When did you catch on that she must have been wearing her glasses? Most people don't have to make it all the way to the end of the story to realize that she can't find her glasses because she has them on. But Marie doesn't get it until the mirror shows her what she looks like. Believe it or not, this is a great analogy for the cause and effect of an assessment.

In order to help a decision maker see the problems within their organization, you must become the mirror. An assessment is the tool to do so. And, in order to convince a decision maker that an assessment is a good step in the first place, you need to understand the way in which they view their world.

There is a bizarre phenomenon that happens within the workplace between leadership and work-related pain. (To clarify, this rarely involves physical pain. Instead, it refers to things that stand in the way of an organization being able to accomplish its mission. There is an element of "pain" felt when this happens. It is often process-driven, and can include things like cumbersome processes, workflow bottlenecks, ineffective cash flow, poor leadership and poor communication.) Some leaders simply cannot see it. Others refuse to see it. And some believe it is just part of doing business. Reasons for this phenomenon range from a reluctance to change, to favoring the status quo, and even sometimes a normalization of workplace pain.

1. Reluctance to Change: The worst reason to do anything is because "that's the way we've always done it." If there is one more phrase that could be stricken permanently from the reference book for socially acceptable human interaction, it should be

this one! When a decision maker is reluctant to change, it provides valuable insight for determining your next steps as a Consultant.

2. Favoring the Status Quo: Someone once said, "It is better to dance with the devil you know." That someone favors the status quo because they fear the unknown. This same personality type utters the phrase, "If it ain't broke, don't fix it." They may be willing to admit there is an issue. But they also tend to be fearful of the level of change necessary to address that issue.

3. Normalization of Workplace Pain: Imagine feeling as though work is supposed to be unnecessarily difficult. These decision makers do! They will happily point out issues, but feel that addressing them somehow makes their employees and coworkers less valuable. As strange as it sounds, this is a very real outlook and you will run into them from time to time!

    Overcome these obstacles by:

    • Downplaying the amount of change that is necessary

- Aligning the Change with organizational or leadership goals
- Ensure that they remain in control of what change, if any, is to take place.
- If you feel risky, it is effective to approach certain personality types with a sense of duty. When it works, they often end up championing the entire process.
- Workplace Statistics

Assessments do something else. It's something every organization strives for. Every year, corporations spend billions of dollars in research and advertising trying to achieve this result; often to no benefit. AUTHENTICITY. Interestingly enough, assessments actually accomplish the task. A properly conducted Assessment enables the sales team to harness the advantage of that sought-after key differentiator: Authenticity.

Few brands have been successful at earning customers through authenticity. Those that have, enjoy a following often described as "cultish." Think of Apple, Starbucks, Lululemon, and Crossfit. Each one of these organizations offers products or services at a higher price than its competitors. In some instances, the product is actually inferior to its competitors. Yet, they continue to harbor a strong level of consumer sentiment in their markets. How is that possible? The answer likely lies in their ability to connect to an authentic desire within the customer. The only way to map to authenticity is to be authentic! No one can coach authenticity, and this is where companies attempting to replicate this level of success often fail. They set out on a quest for consumer data studies and marketing campaign bids in order to create a message that is perceived as authentic. What an oxy-moron! The concept of creating a message of "authenticity" based on what studies show consumers want is not authentic at all! And today's astute consumer can see right through every bit of it.

Action is what distinguishes a good marketing campaign from genuine authenticity. The companies mentioned above don't advertise in a way that is designed to map to consumer sentiment. They create consumer sentiment. Apple is all about simplicity. So, people who feel cluttered by all the "stuff" they are surrounded by in their daily lives are naturally drawn to a company who creates simple and elegantly designed products. Apple doesn't sell phones, they sell an experience. Guess what Starbucks sells? An experience. They are so sold-out on the idea of serving good coffee (not just coffee) that in 2008, Starbucks closed their doors for an entire day so every barista in the company could practice the art of brewing and presenting the perfect cup of coffee. Who does that? A coffee company who is truly concerned about your coffee experience. Lululemon caters to those who wish to live a holistic, healthy lifestyle. Where Starbucks and Apple advertisements are nearly everywhere you look, Lululemon relies on almost entirely word-of-mouth marketing. Talk about a cult following! Lululemon isn't about making clothes to sell to those who wish to live a healthy lifestyle. Lululemon is about the experience of living a healthy lifestyle. There's that word again! Their understanding of healthy goes far beyond the gym. They cater to the healthy body and the healthy mind. Their bags and store signage often display positive, optimistic, healthy messages. They don't do this because some marketing team told them gym rats love to be inspired, but because their corporation genuinely believes a healthy lifestyle goes beyond physical fitness. And there are clearly lots of people with disposable income willing to pay $100 for leggings who agree. Those people wouldn't be caught dead in a pair of comparable $40 Nike leggings. Why? Because it doesn't map to who they are.

Some of you might be looking at that brand list and making the false assumption that authenticity is a yuppie, millennial kind of thing. Think again. In 2008, a relatively unknown Senator from Illinois ran on a campaign of change and became the first

African American President of the United States. In 2016, a complete political outsider and TV Personality ran on a campaign based entirely on the fact that he was a political outsider and became the 45th President of the United States. It is certainly safe to say both of these individuals are drastically different. It is also likely safe to say that you voted for one and not the other. What is interesting is that both of these Presidents ran campaigns based on authenticity. Both Presidents ran against a field of candidates with more experience and both were seen as the unlikely candidate in early polling. They had radically different messages. But their messages were authentic. And in both elections, those authentic messages moved voters to the polls in large numbers.

It's not totally impossible to imagine your corporation developing a cult following of its own. It happens. But, it is rare. It is also unlikely for an existing organization to shift gears and suddenly spend the time and resources necessary to devote to its own authenticity. However, whether they do or do not makes no impact on the fact that they employ a team of very real and very authentic people directly responsible for their corporate image. ...You.

Sales is already geared slightly toward authenticity. As proof, imagine the organization you work for suddenly had a load of complaints. Turns out, the product or service you've been selling is terrible. People hate it. It is not as it was advertised. And they are angry. Because of this, the morale in the sales office is way down. Leadership is agitated and exhausted from working overtime to deal with managing refunds, warranties and the public relations nightmare. But, sales quotas haven't changed. Your pay structure has not been altered, and so your job is still to go out every day and represent an organization whose products and services are not good. Can you do it? Would you do it?

For even the most stalwart sales veteran, this scenario is typically the kiss of death. Why? Because it makes selling completely disingenuous. Brian Tracy, author of "The Psychology of Selling" wrote that more than half of a person's ability to sell comes from an enthusiasm and excitement about the product or service they are selling. Remove authenticity and you've literally drained half of their ability. The flip side to this scenario is to question what happens when you enhance authenticity by providing a quality product or service introduced through a genuine sales method. Magic.

If today's decision maker is seeking authenticity, what could be more authentic than you expressing genuine interest in them? That's one more benefit to Consultative Selling!

So, what should an assessment involve? Here's the million-dollar question. And, the answer is not a simple one. It depends upon your organization's marketable output. In order to know how to help a customer, you must understand your organization's value proposition and match it against 3 things:

1. Their current status.
2. Their future plans.
3. Their biggest pain point.

For example, it does little good to facilitate a financial assessment on an organization if you are an IT service provider. However, you can get a clearer picture for the best way to structure your IT service to meet THEIR NEEDS based upon the effectiveness of their current contract. That would be part of an assessment of their current status. If they are reluctant to show pricing for what they are currently paying for something, tell them they can redact it. You're not here to compete on price, anyway. You are here to bring value.

"Price is only an issue in the absence of value"

It also helps to document. Analyzing someone's current contract, invoice or portfolio design is a fantastic component of a proper assessment. It also helps to provide you a pathway for building value and differentiation. Depending upon what your marketable output is, even pictures of employees aren't out of the question. Imagine delivering a Summary Report showing pictures of each employee with their current Insurance Benefit enrollments listed, with a breakdown showing cost to employee, cost to company and an efficiency score based upon how often they use the insurance. Wouldn't that be impressive? Pictures are an effective tool to demonstrate a familiarity with their organization and a reference to demonstrate where they can go.

While assessing the current status of an organization, be insatiably curious. Even though you might have a list of 10 or 20 questions to answer, it is important to follow the lead of the customer. For example, if you're selling vehicle fleets to a large service organization and they tell you they've always provided gas allowance in the past, find out why. Even though you know all the reasons why a fleet is better than gas allowances, the assessment is not the place to share your wealth of knowledge.

Instead, chase them down the rabbit hole with a string of questions until you understand every in and out of their current perspective on vehicle fleets. If you're prompted for advice during an assessment, respond by providing a depth of experience and a willingness to wait for the right time to answer. Something like: "First, let me explain that you're not alone.

Plenty of leaders, just like you, have similar concerns. The good news is that by the end of this assessment, I'll have a great background of information to be able to provide you with sound advice based around your organization."

Future goals are, without a doubt, the most fun part of any assessment. This is where you get a great feel for the direction a buyer is headed in their life, or where the leadership is taking the organization. Understanding their future can also make you an immediate valuable asset during the delivery of the Summary Report when you include a list of opportunities to take advantage of and pitfalls to avoid as they plan for their future. It aligns you, your organization, and your marketable output with their future in a method called parallel synergy. Creating parallel synergy is what makes relationships sticky. It's the reason the old sales dude gets calls from his customers, rather than the other way around. They know he understands where they've been and where they are going. He's the only one they will call, because he's the only one who knows them that well. An astounding level of trust can be generated simply by asking an organization what they hope to accomplish in the future, or what their next project is.

Finally, there's the break point question. Every person has something they worry about. And you will be surprised how quickly they will share it with you. Break point questions are the most important question in the entire assessment. Because they are typically pointed and direct, they should be saved for the latter portion of the assessment. Sitting down with a decision maker for the first time and rattling off a question about what their biggest headache is would likely not end well.

The leader of a small midwestern-based consulting firm frequently used the saying, "That's like picking out drapes while the house is on fire!" It was his way of pointing out to a client that they had bigger issues than the ones they are currently addressing. Learning a buyer's break point prevents you from doing the same thing. If their biggest concern is cash flow, you know to present your marketable output in payments or smaller phases. Whereas, if their biggest issue is an upcoming election, you might probe that one a bit more to eventually come to realize they don't like taxes. Consult with their tax attorney or CFO to find out what their recommendation would be for presenting your solutions. Showing up to the Summary Report with a recommendation from their trusted advisor can sometimes elevate you to that level of trust quickly.

Assessments 101

Conducting an assessment should be a ritualized, organized and well-communicated event. Here are a few pointers to help you conduct a proper assessment:

- Send a calendar invite to all who will be interviewed during your assessment
- Call the leader the day prior to the assessment to remind them (do not ask if it is still ok to conduct your assessment – just remind them)
- Arrive promptly and hand the leader or leadership team a typed schedule printed on your letterhead with THEIR logo at the top
- Begin by asking what it is they hope to accomplish with the assessment
- Conduct interviews privately
- Take lots of notes
- Do a walk-through of their facilities
- Take pictures

Asking the right questions is sometimes difficult. This is especially true if it is an industry or market vertical you've not worked with before. Here are 12 sample questions to help you get on the right track: (please adjust these questions according to your organization's marketable output)

1. What do you hope to accomplish today?
2. Tell me how you became the "title" of "organization".
3. I've done a bit of research, so I know what I think you do. But, tell me in your own words what "organization" does?
4. Where do your sales typically come from?
5. Who are your ideal customers and how do you reach them?
6. Do you have a diversified customer base, or do you primarily serve a small few, large customers?
7. Where are you leading this company in the next 5-10 years?
8. Do you prefer to outsource as much as possible, or do as much as possible?
9. Who do you rely on to make decisions?
10. What process goes very well here?
11. What process needs improvement?
12. What keeps you up at night?

Your goal during any assessment is to be insatiably curious. Avoid providing advice during an assessment. Instead, ask follow-up questions to the main basic questions to go deeper with the customer. This gives you an even better understanding of the organization, the decision maker, and their needs scenario. As an example, let's assume the decision maker enlightens you with the fact that they rely upon their COO to help make decisions (question 9, above). That alone, is fantastic information to have because you now know who needs to be part of any Summary Report delivery or Proposal meeting. However, to gain a better perspective on the decision making dynamic of their leadership, take the customer deeper by asking a follow-up question. You should ask something like, "Explain the role your COO plays for you in that process." Now, you not only know who is involved, but you know why they are involved. Knowing this can help you be prepared to present information to the customer in such a way that you set them up for success in resolving their issues with your solutions.

<u>Settling in with Their Pain</u>

Every buyer and every organization experiences pain. You are likely aware of different needs scenarios within your own organization! Listen for it as you are performing an initial assessment with the decision maker you've set the appointment with. You will hear the moment the pain arises. It's an inflection in their voice, or a heavy sigh. In some cases, they will just come straight at you with it, verbally. No matter how it gets there, be prepared for it.

There is something within our human nature that makes us uncomfortable with someone else's uncomfortable-ness. Learning to be ok with someone else's pain is a key factor in any consultative role. It enhances empathetic communication; a powerful relationship building skill. So, while our tendency may be to run when someone else is squeamish; learn to settle in with it, instead. Stop everything else and get on their level with what they are expressing. You will find that when you become an astute practitioner of empathy your body language will often even mirror theirs.

Here is an example of how that conversation might go. Let's say you work as an account representative for a marketing firm. You are on the quest for new clientele and are working to gain their entire business; not just re-designing logos. So, you are conducting an initial assessment using the 12 questions above. When you ask the obvious market-driven questions about where their customers come from, the decision maker doesn't reveal much in the way of pain. But when you get to the question about where they see themselves going in the next 5-10 years, she pauses, sighs, looks down and says, "I'm not sure."

Your brain should trigger a pain alert right then and there! Time to go deeper with her. Let's dig this out. Make eye contact and reveal your concern in a way that lets her know you are genuinely concerned. "That's a surprising answer. Tell me more."

"You see, we have a new competitor in the market. They came in with lower pricing and our business has now become marginalized. We are having to compete on price and our margins have dropped by 15% across the board."

This is where it gets real. Settle in with her and say something simple, then prompt to go deeper. "That's not good. What solutions have you tried?"

"We are at a bit of a loss. Our market value used to be that our products were all manufactured locally and came with a solid replacement warranty. To start outsourcing products from somewhere else would be to go against the very foundation of our company. We also looked at downsizing, but we run pretty lean as it is. Plus, laying off good employees just because we can't compete didn't seem right."

Remember that part about settling in with the pain? Here's where it happens. "It must have been really difficult to have those conversations." Now, you sit. You sit in silence while you wait for them to confirm what you already know.

"It was."

At this point, the marketer has options:

1. Champion the decision maker – This tool is either incredibly effective or just fluff. You decide whether or not it makes sense at the time based, primarily, off the personality of the person(s) you're having the conversation with.

2. Move on to the next point – Good job. You dug out the pain, settled in with it, now it's time to move on.

3. Propose to resolve the pain – Cut to the chase and forget the rest of the assessment. It's time to move into close mode.

<u>To Charge or not to Charge</u>

Statistically, the average organization will spend $50,000 on a consultation. Today, most sales teams are accustomed to begging for sales appointments, rather than charging for them. The idea of telling a customer they will need to pay in order to meet with a member of our sales team sounds silly, brash and doomed-to-fail. If all your organization intends to do is continue to train "traditional sales people," then you are correct. But, you're reading the book. So, it is probably safe to assume you're at least curious about making a shift into a consultative sales approach. This means your will spend more time developing a client, rather than selling to them. It will create larger sales, but can slow the initial sales cycle. It also means you are now in the business of providing advice within your area of expertise. Professionals who provide advice have been charging us to do so for years! Think of attorneys, accountants, engineers, etc. ...and consultants! Because of this widely accepted business practice, organizations who make the shift to consultative sales often end up creating an additional revenue stream from their assessments. Determining what to charge for your assessments or consultations is a combination of many factors, including:

- Geographic Location
- Your Marketable Output
- Customer's Organizational Size
- Number of Locations
- Detail of Assessment
- Size and Scope of Summary Report

Curious as to how to have the conversation? When transitioning to Consultative Sales, create a structure for a low-end (or free) brief assessment and a paid full assessment. This provides you with the greatest amount of flexibility in the field. After conducting an initial assessment (using the questions above), you should learn more about the organizational needs scenario of your potential customer. If you've done your job correctly, they have opened up to you and you now know a few major pain-points they are experiencing.

Use those points to make the offer to dig deeper into the issue with a paid assessment.

"What we've done today has been productive. It has given me some insight to bring back relevant solutions to you and your team that I believe can help. But, given the complexity of your organization, I'd feel better by making certain we have turned over every stone. Your organization would benefit from a more robust assessment."

Wait for their response. Usually, the decision maker will request clarification or more detail.

"It's the old iceberg illustration, right? What we did today in the time we shared was literally scratch the surface. It brought some issues to the top, but we honestly can't see the other 80% that's below the surface, yet. What I'm asking for is your permission to explore that part. Your (insert primary issue here) may be the problem, or it may simply be a symptom of another problem. It's worth it to me to find the answer to that question. What do you think?"

Typically, the next part involves things like what they get in a paid assessment and the price. And that part is entirely up to you! But this gets the conversation started!

In closing, a great assessment is conducted by combining Conscientious Leadership skills with insatiable curiosity. Here are a few things to remember:

- First, try conducting an Initial Assessment to see if a full Consult makes sense.
- Ask lots of questions. Your job is to be the most curious person in the room!
- Learn their decision making process. This helps you down the road.
- Consider paid full assessments if you feel the situation warrants it.

"A statement closes a door. A question opens it."

Chapter Five : Key Points

- Traditional Sales uses a scattered, craps-table approach to selling
- Consultative Sales uses Assessments as a way to help the decision maker see issues in their own organization in an objective way
- Leadership can sometimes be reluctant to address work-related pain due to:
  - Reluctance to Change
  - Favoring the Status Quo
  - Normalization
- Assessments add the value of "Authenticity" by creating a genuine customer experience
- Assessments should provide insight into 3 generalities:
  - Their Current Status
  - Their Future Plans
  - Their Biggest Pain Point
- "Price is only an issue in the absence of value."
- When a pain is expressed, settle in with it. This enhances empathetic communication.
- 71% of all businesses will hire a consultant in 2019 and expect to spend over $50,000.
- You can charge for assessments, if it makes sense.
- "A statement closes a door, a question opens it."

Chapter 6

Analysis

"We've got to break them out of this losing streak!" shouted the tiny man from across the room. They had just lost another game, and the pressure from the parents, players and administration was piling up on the coaching staff.

Allen examined his scrawny assistant coach. Two small dark eyes peered back at him through wire-rimmed glasses. He noticed that when the assistant spoke, the words seemed to barely escape his narrow lips. The assistant droned on for a few more sentences before staring at his somewhat oblivious supervisor.

"You're the head coach! Aren't you going to do something?" he pleaded.

"Yes." Said Allen. He glanced at the trophies scattered around the room. Over a decade of State Championships won, and now they have a losing record. He knew why. Their conference was changed. Gone were the days of being the most feared team in the sport. The team had become complacent in the last few years, but the shift had somehow made it worse. Now they were lackadaisical and unmotivated. Practices were filled with the same drills and conditioning that made them successful. But the players didn't perform the drills. They simply "did" the drills. They were going through the motions, and Allen knew it. If they were ever going to break out of this cycle, he had to make a point.

"Send notice to the parents and the players. Show up next Friday in a suit and tie."

The assistant looked up from his phone where he had been frantically typing. His fingers seemed to freeze in the blue light of the screen. He titled his head forward as if he misheard the head coach. "But we don't have a game next Friday."

"I know." Allen replied. "I'm doing something."

The players looked sharp beneath the orange sky that Friday evening as they lined up to get on the bus in their jackets & ties. Excitement filled the air as theories about what they were doing and where they were going were tossed about. Allen smiled and greeted them. Whenever he was asked about their destination, he would nod and say, "You're never going to forget it."

When the players were all seated, he stood at the front of the aisle dividing long rows of seats. Silence fell among the players as hope filled their expressions for some sort of clue as to where they were going, and why.

"Gentlemen, I hope you brought your appetites." He said.

"Yes sir," rang a few responses from random spots among the seated athletes.

"I'm always hungry, Coach." Said a particularly enthusiastic Ray Wilson. At 6' 6" and breaking 300 pounds, he was easily their biggest player. He was a senior this year and had also earned a spot as their team captain.

"Ray, I expected that from you." Allen quipped as laughter spread among the team.

"Gentlemen, this is no ordinary dinner. So, I expect each of you to be at your best while we are here. Remember who we represent." With that, he turned to the bus driver. "Let's move." He said and began to sit in his customary seat at the front.

"One more thing!" Allen shouted as he stopped in a squatting position, turning his attention back to his players. "No matter what happens, you aren't allowed to say anything to the wait staff. Got that?"

"Yes sir!" Came the replies from the bus. Though their responses were affirmation, their faces showed confusion at the bizarre request.

"What if I need seconds?" Ray leaned forward and whispered to the players seated in front of him, jokingly.

The thirty-minute drive seemed to take hours. As they arrived in the final moments of daylight, the beams of light from the bus illuminated an unmistakable building and recognition exploded around the bus like popcorn in a skillet. "The Governor's Mansion!" Emotion and noise rose together as the bus came to a hissing stop beneath the large stairway leading to the double-door entrance to the Mansion.

Allen stood up and the clamor stopped. "You are all aware that the Governor and I played on this team when we were your age." He said. "Tonight, you are his special guests. Just *remember, be at your best, remember who you represent, and no talking to the wait staff."*

Inside the great dining hall, the tables were lined with fine linen cloths and shiny, perfectly positioned silverware sparkled beneath crystal chandeliers. Chargers bearing the team's mascot were set. As the players were seated a bell rang and a fleet of wait staff whisked around the room setting plates and glasses. Their outfits were perfectly pressed with black jackets and silk bow ties.

Allen took a moment to glance around the room, taking in the players' exhilaration. He withheld a chuckle as he noticed his pin-head assistant coach practically giddy over the whole experience. For a moment, the assistant gave him a nod as if to say he agreed with the decision to bring them to the Governor's Mansion for a motivational field trip. Allen raised his empty glass and smirked.

As quickly as they appeared, the waiters were all gone. Music began playing from a lone violinist in the corner of the hall. Suddenly, they all reappeared with white cloths draped across one arm and a pitcher in the other. Allen watched as they went from player to player pouring the pitchers. And he smiled as the young men reacted to the fact that their pitchers were empty. The waiters acted as if nothing was amiss as they fussed over the team until everyone had been served. They disappeared again from the room.

"Hey, I know we aren't supposed to say anything to them, but they forgot to put drink in the drinks." An athlete across the table from Ray whispered to him.

"I know, dude." Said Ray. "Maybe it's like a joke or something."

The wait staff appeared in the hall once again. This time with silver serving platters containing a mysterious meal beneath a shiny dome top.

"Foooooood." Ray jokingly whispered. His tablemates chuckled.

The waiters moved in near perfect choreographed rhythm as they delicately removed plates from the trays and placed them on the custom chargers in front of the athletes. Empty.

Allen could feel all 46 glances coming from each player across the dining hall. It was everything he could do not to react. He sat, content, with his empty glass and empty plate in front of him. The assistant coach began to rise from his seat, but Allen quickly motioned for him to sit. He waited.

"Maybe you should find out what's going on, man." A player mentioned to Ray.

"Coach said not to say anything." He responded.

"Yeah. He told us not to say anything to the waiters. But you should go ask Coach what's going on!" he whispered.

The wooden chair made a loud bark as Ray scooted it back. His large frame caught the eye of every team member as he made his way over to where their coach was seated. The room was silent. They all watched as the two men exchanged words no one else could hear. After a few moments, Ray nodded his head and made his way back to his seat. His chair groaned again as he scooted it back under the table. He stared at his plate, avoiding eye contact with any of his fellow teammates.

Allen stood. His players turned to face him.

"What's the problem?" He asked.

No one answered.

"Everyone did what they were supposed to do." He said. "The hall was prepared for you. The room was set as it should be. The waiters performed flawlessly. No one dropped anything. No one moved out of turn. No one skipped a glass or a plate. They served every person here."

"Served us nothing." The player at Ray's table retorted sarcastically.

"What's that?" Coach asked.

"He was just saying they didn't actually serve us anything, sir." Ray responded.

"Well that depends on your definition of serving, doesn't it?" Allen replied. "The wait staff poured the pitchers. They set the plates. They went through the motions and gave you perfect execution. But you're all upset because it's not the action that was the problem. It was the substance. It doesn't matter that someone pours a pitcher into a glass if there's nothing in the pitcher. Being served an empty plate does nothing for someone who is hungry."

"You guys look the part. You've got the right size to play. You've got the right equipment. A big beautiful stadium. You've got fans in the stands. And I watch this team day-in-and-day-out perform drills, review tape, perfect plays and condition your bodies to compete. You're doing all the right things. But you're lacking in substance. There's no fight in you. There's no passion. There's no meat on your plate. You're just out there pouring empty pitchers every day."

The door to the great hall opened and the players all gasped as the Governor entered the room. "I am hungry. I'm hungry for a win!" he said as he pumped a fist adorned with his championship ring. Rushing in from behind him came a stream of waiters with trays of 16oz sirloins cooked to perfection and pitchers of ice-cold sweet tea.

"Now let's eat!"

You've spent the time acquiring the client, earning their trust, and you've now spent hours or possibly even days assessing their current status. The stage is set for a beautiful solution-based sale where you get to be the hero by delivering a win-win scenario for their organization and yours. But, truthfully, this is where most consultative sales go awry. Getting to this point can become so routine over time that it feels almost habitual. Don't let it.

Don't waste an amazing opportunity by just going through the motions. In the story above, the team was doing all the right things. But they weren't executing with any substance. Everything was being done at a surface-value level.

You undoubtedly went through some training on your organization and on the products / services offered by your organization. You know the marketable output because you were hired to get out there and market it. So, the chances are high that on multiple occasions during the assessment, you knew exactly what solutions you could provide for them based upon their perceived pain. But, is rushing back to your desk and jotting those things down immediately really any form of analysis? To jump through analysis without really studying it carefully isn't just lacking in substance. It is also costly:

It will cost you time. If the only level of analysis you give to this process is a surface-level knee-jerk aha-moment that recalled a phrase you heard during your products/services orientation; you might as well have just gone in for a traditional sale. That's what the old model is based on, right? Probe until you hear a sales trigger, then jump in there, latch on and don't let go until someone has signed something. If you try to skirt analysis, it was a waste of your time to get to this point in the process.

It will cost you money. A thorough analysis means you will statistically come back recommending two to four times the average number of solutions as a traditional sale. Short changing the analysis means you are also short on change.

It will cost valuable relationships. The statistics on Consultative Sales are staggering. It is how today's business leaders want to be sold to. This method opens doors Traditional Sales methods get you banned from for life. If you walk them through this process, it will make them hungry for results. You can't provide the substance of that result if you are just going through the motions. They will know it, and you will ruin a potential life-long relationship.

Name 3 things more important to a sales professional than time, money and relationships!

Caffeine may come in as a close number 4. But for most sales pros, those are the three metrics by which they measure their professional lives. This step is so vital that it will impact all 3!

5 Types of Common Analysis

1. Threading Analysis

In almost every crime movie ever made, there is a moment where someone puts news clippings and pictures on a cork board or a map. Sometimes, they literally even "thread" the storyline together using red yarn. This is where the tactic gets its name.

Threading involves laying out the assessment data in such a way that it begins to tell its own story. Most often, threading analysis will be the type of analysis used from interviews you conducted during your assessment. Look for similar statements or issues presented by more than one employee, manager, or leadership team member. Write each occurrence down on a separate sheet of paper along with who said it and their role within the organization. Note any nuance made that might give you enhanced insight into the common theme.

Problems within organizations are often systemic in nature. It works a lot like your own body. Have you ever wondered why you can go to the doctor for a sprained ankle and they still check your vitals? The physician is not just focused on the sprained ankle. They are also making sure the reason you sprained it is just incidental and that the ankle isn't a symptom of a larger, systemic problem. A good consultant works like a good physician. It is your job to read past the surface-level and into the system of the organization.

For example, let's say that multiple members of management within a hospital mention that it is difficult to keep good employees. It's pretty tempting to mark that one at a surface-level and move on. High employee turnover. Your people aren't happy. Check. Moving on! But for a moment, let's consider some of the variables that can affect employee turnover:

- High stress
- Financial / Low pay
- Feeling unappreciated
- Inadequate employee training
- Environmental factors
- Inadequate management training
- Poor benefits

That list could go on, and there are probably a few you could add from your own experience. But this list does present an interesting component to threading. Since it could be any of these, how do you know which one is the primary cause? You don't. And it might be disadvantageous for you to narrow it down. Often, leadership teams will agree on multiple contributors to a common issue. It is a good idea, however, to see if further threading can help you narrow it down by process of elimination. Use what is left to create a list of the top probable reasons for the issue THAT YOU CAN ADDRESS. There is no reason to include environmental factors if you're not an interior designer. It is a known fact that brown walls contribute to dissatisfaction in employees. But that is only a finding you can address if you have paint! However, there are a few on that list you can address if you sell group insurance, process management software or corporate training solutions. The point is to make sure you are threading through systemic issues you can provide the solutions to resolve.

2. Situational Contradiction Analysis

Have you ever met someone who wanted to be more fit, but refused to establish a workout routine? How about someone who complained all the time, but never worked a plan to change their situation? If you answered yes to either of those questions, congratulations! You understand Situational Contradiction.

You'll be amazed at how often this occurs in business. During an Assessment, leadership may place great emphasis on investment in technology. But, then, you find out their off-site employees (field workers, sales team, delivery, etc.) are filling paper forms. Often, this is simply a result of oversight. Your ability to draw this simple conclusion in an Analysis creates a case for change using their own perspective on what is important. Finding a customer with a mission statement is a perfect setup for a Situational Contradiction Analysis. The whole purpose of a mission statement is to act as a litmus by which an organization measures everything it does. So, any business practice, purchase, or otherwise that is contradictory to the mission statement of an organization presents an immediate cause for change. The choices are to change their current business practice, or to adopt a revised mission statement. Which would you choose?

As an example, a client's mission statement says they use "the most efficient technology possible" to perform the work of the organization. You walk into their building and see paper everywhere, old yellowed monitor screens, vehicle fleets from 15 years ago, and cables dangling from holes punched through ceilings to network their technology. Taking note of this during your analysis is key to their future success as an organization, and to your success as a consultant to them.

3. Frequency Analysis

Leadership interviews can sometimes leave you feeling like you're living in "Groundhog's Day" with Bill Murray. Here's why: well-run organizations operate by systems. However, because of the interconnected nature of systems, issues tend to be systemic. Therefore, problems experienced in one part of the system (department/business process) are noticed or reflected in other parts of the system. A disorganized or understaffed Accounts Payable Department can literally hijack every other department's productivity. The same goes for issues in the field (sales / service).

You will know when this is an issue because you will hear it during your leadership interviews in the Assessment. The majority of the interview you are conducting ends up sounding much like the ones before it. And this is Frequency.

The best thing about Frequency is that it is an easily scorable component to your analysis. If you spoke to 10 managers and 7 of them mentioned issues related to Accounts Payable, then you know there is a 70% Frequency of that occurrence across the organization. It makes a solid presentation to list issues in order of frequency when presenting your Summary to a client.

Frequency Analysis is a helpful tool for highlighting systemic issues prevalent in the organization. Assigning a score to the Analysis helps the client to prioritize needs and provides guidance to your Phased Delivery process.

4. Reporting Tools Analysis

If you are doing anything worthwhile, it is likely someone before you has also done it. The advantage to you from that scenario is in the form of a Reporting Tool. Sometimes these are available at no cost (Internet Speed Tests, for example). If not, paying for the subscription to a reporting tool is worth consideration.

Graphs and tables with organized information have a way of breaking up an analysis. Not to mention, you don't usually have to do much more than input the data if you use a pre-existing tool.

Another benefit to using a reporting tool is that the analysis is from a neutral, third-party. When your analysis lines up with theirs, it has a way of building instant trust with the client. It's almost a stamp of approval that you are not just trying to "sell them something." You're there because they have a problem and you have the resources to bring them solutions to that problem. Free tool or not, don't underestimate the power of a reporting tool. It should never be the entire reason you're recommending a solution. But, it can often be the component to Analysis that cements the client's need for change.

5. Inventory Analysis

A picture is worth a thousand words. As you're conducting a walk-through during the Assessment, take pictures. If what you are doing in Consultative Sales is making the "case" for why an organization should make a change, then a catalogue of relevant pictures should become your exhibits.

Using the scenario of the mis-matched mission "efficient technology" statement, showing their own words across a collage of photos showing out-of-date technology makes a profound statement without you having to say a word about it. All you need to do is share with them that this is an example of Situational Contradiction, then provide the definition.

Inventory is also helpful to have in the form of lists and specifications or details. For example, the following list of employees have enrolled in insurance benefits which cost the company "x", the employee "x", and are used "x" times per year.

When offering a competing quote or product, you know where you stand BEFORE you present. Make the case for why they should change relative to what they are currently doing. This makes an ally out of your competition. How often do you get to do that?

Analysis is something that varies greatly with the type of industry you are in and the market vertical you are selling to. There are other forms of Analysis, but experience has shown these to be the most powerful in setting up a point. What is that point? Ultimately, it is to say:

"You made a great decision in allowing (or hiring!) me to perform an assessment for your organization. Based upon the findings we gathered from your organization, we can confidently recommend that there are changes that need to be made."

Chapter Six : Key Points

- Diligence and substance are the keys to good Analysis
- Rushing or jumping to conclusions can cost you:
  - Time
  - Money
  - Valuable Relationships
- 5 Types of Common Analysis
  - Threading
  - Situational Contradiction
  - Frequency
  - Reporting Tools
  - Inventory

Chapter 7

Summary Report Prep & Presentation

This Chapter is dedicated to former NASA astronaut, Captain Sonny Carter. Sonny was a Georgia-born Eagle Scout who went on to graduate as a physician from the Emory University School of Medicine in 1973. While he attended medical school, Sonny played professional soccer for the Atlanta Chiefs in the North American Soccer League. After graduating, he entered the US Navy's flight surgeon school. Eventually, his love of flight drove him to enter flight school and he was declared a Naval Aviator in 1978. He was assigned as the senior medical officer aboard the aircraft carrier, *USS Forrestal*. In March of 1979, he was reassigned as a fighter pilot, flying F-4 Phantoms with Marine Fighter Attack Squadron 333 (VMFA-333). In September of 1982, Sonny attended US Navy Fighter Weapons School (TOPGUN). During his time in the Navy, he logged over 3,000 flying hours and 160 carrier landings. Cpt. Sonny Carter became a NASA Astronaut in June of 1985 and was assigned Mission Specialist on Space Shuttle flight crews. In 1989, he served as the EVA (Extra-vehicular Activity) Representative on NASA flight STS-33 aboard the Space Shuttle *Discovery*. It was NASA's first flight following the Space Shuttle *Challenger* disaster in 1988.

At the age of 6, I met my second hero, Sonny Carter (my Dad will always be my first). Sonny's record of achievement and excellence serves as an example for those who strive to be beyond typical, and to make a true impact on this world. Unfortunately, Sonny's life was unexpectedly cut short in the crash of Atlantic Southeast Airlines Flight 2311 in 1991. But, not before our lives briefly intertwined. My Dad recruited and hosted Captain Sonny Carter to a corporate event. In spite of everything he had accomplished, Sonny was a kind, humble and humorous soul whose story has inspired me to assume anything worth dreaming is worth accomplishing.

Sara Summers glanced at the thermal long johns neatly laid across the table as she entered the prep-room. Protocol requires that she wear only NASA approved fabric. Everything matters in space. "96% chance of mission success," she reminded herself. Statistics made her feel better. Math made her feel better.

The former Navy pilot reviewed her physique in the mirror to her left. To her, it was a visual representation of preparation. Readiness. As if somehow years of training were encapsulated in every sinew of her taut reflection. She appeared more machine than woman. But she was a woman. And she was a Mom.

"Sally." She said softly as she twisted a tendril of her own light brown hair. She saw her daughter in the face staring back from the mirror as she recalled their long hug the night before. Sara always thought she would have a son. But when her daughter was born, she named her after Sally Ride, the first female astronaut. And like her mother, Sally Summers also had dreams of exploring the deep reaches of space.

"Sixty-two" she whispered into her daughter's ear as they held one another.

"Sixty-two" Sally replied softly.

Sixty-two was how many miles Sara had to pilot the ship until it was free of Earth's atmosphere. For Sally, the number represented how far her Mom was going to be away from her. Earlier that week, they had rented a convertible, drove 62 miles, and placed a heart shaped stone beside the road. On their way home they stopped at a fruit stand and shared a Georgia peach. Deep in thoughts of summer peaches and road trips, Sara jumped as the heavy metal door to her prep-room clanged open.

"Captain Summers, I'm Major Lucas and we are your prep team for today's mission." The man said in a formal tone. He and his team were wearing traditional NASA jump suits. Everything from here-on would be a well-rehearsed strategic dance designed to get a 110 lb. woman into a 200 lb. space suit.

From her time in the military, to her engagement with the space program, Sara had become an expert in the pathway to flawless performance. Planning leads to Preparation. Preparation leads to Practice. Practice leads to Proficiency. Proficiency leads to Performance. And Performance is what gets you back home. Everything that was going to happen today had followed that same pathway. But today was no longer about Practice. It was time to Perform.

Sara glanced at her forearm before sliding her arm into the long sleeve. Her daughter had used a pen to trace the number 62 on her arm so that she would have a reminder of home during her 90 day space flight. In reality, the International Space Station was over 200 miles from Earth. But at 6 years old, 62 seemed a much easier number for Sally to understand.

As Major Lucas made the final adjustment to Sara's helmet, he tapped it on top and said, "God Speed, Captain Summers."

Sara nodded as she began the 37 steps it took for her to get to the elevator. She passed a small crowd of reporters and dignitaries. No flash pictures were allowed. No unknown elements. No unnecessary risks. She provided them with one conciliatory wave before focusing her gaze on the elevator. The operator inside greeted her with the salute customary of a formal Naval officer. He didn't offer any formalities, but simply said, "Next stop, Zero Deck."

The sun sparkled across the ocean as the 135 ft. ride to her shuttle access deck came to a stop. The view was magnificent. Sara tried to quell her feelings and focus on the mission, but a smile slipped through as all her professional accomplishments came flooding to her through a funnel that led to this moment. "10,000 hours to make an expert and you're almost 4 times that.

You earned this moment." she thought as the euphoria of accomplishment briefly consumed her.

Ahead was her ship, the Aura. It was the first of its kind. Aerospace experts, news media and space fanatics fawned over its unique design. Artificial intelligence and simple features enabled the slender craft to be piloted by a one-member crew. Powered by nuclear propulsion, the ship was able to forego the traditional attachments formerly used to hold fuel and various propulsion engines. It was streamlined and efficient. To her, it was beautiful.

Media outlets praised the moment as the "first time" anyone would ever pilot this ship. Sara laughed every time she heard or read the ridiculous statement. "It's incendiary nonsense." She bemused. "I've flown the Aura on this exact mission through hundreds of different scenarios for the last 3 years!"

The simulator for the Aura was a perfect replica of the craft's pointed nose cone. Each time she simulated a flight, the scenario was different. But everything else remained the same. The toggles, switches, and buttons were always in the same place. The clinical metallic smell of artificial air never changed. The consistent pressure provided by her seat harness always gave her the same sense of security. And the primary steps she's performed tens of thousands of times - both in her mind and in the simulator - that get her to her destination and back again are the same.

Sally watched the large monitor in the control room as her Mother disappeared through the Aura's cockpit hatch door. She was proud of her Mom. Everyone at school knew who her Mom was, and they had all stood and cheered the day she came to school to talk about her journey. But, Sally was also scared. Several times she snuck out of her bed at night to listen to her parents talk. She remembered the first time she heard fear in her Father's voice. She remembered the things her Mother shared to calm him.

"This is a historic event in American spaceflight," the man on the TV said. The launch was being broadcast live all over the world, including in a corner of the control room launch monitor. "A tribute to modern technology and the bravery of the extraordinary men and women of NASA's Aura program." He continued. "And we are proud to bring you live and exclusive coverage of the Aura's first flight."

"It's not untested, John." Sara assured her husband as they sat in the two leather club chairs in their home office. "Every component of the Aura has been tested. I have been tested. I've literally done this blindfolded." Sally peered around the corner on her hands and knees to see what was going to happen next.

Her Father put his drink down on the table between them and reached his hand out to touch her Mom's.

"You, Sara, are the only component of this mission I understand. And you are the only part of this mission I trust."

"Sixty-two." Sara said to John.

"Sixty-two." He replied.

"Sixty-two." Sally whispered from the dark hallway, before crawling down the hallway back to her room.

That memory made the most significant impact on Sally's understanding of her Mom's journey. Her Mom had been tested. And she knew that meant her Mom would win. So did her Dad. She now laughed with them whenever the news sensationalized the Aura's flight as though it was the first. It wasn't. Her Mom had done this a lot over the past 3 years, and she could even do it with her eyes closed.

"Mission Control requesting Ready-Launch." The voice rang out simultaneously through the control room and in Sara's helmet.

"Initiating Ready-Launch sequence." Came Sara's reply. Sally's heart began to race as her Mom's comment echoed through the large room filled with people intensely focused on the screens in front of them.

Sara flew through the next movements almost robotically. Her breathing was calm. Her mind was steady. "Aura to Mission Control. Ready-Launch sequence complete," she said. Then she sat back and waited for the countdown.

"Aura this is Mission Control. God Speed, Captain Summers." Jim Birch, Director of the Aura space program spoke to wish his star pilot well.

"Just another day at the office, Jim." Sally replied, causing Jim and the control room to chuckle.

"Mission Control initiate Countdown to Launch." Jim ordered.

As the countdown ticked down to zero, Sara listened attentively. She heard no wavering in the voice speaking through her headset. That was a good sign. She also began preparing for her next launch movements.

The Aura rumbled beneath her as its atomic engines began to build the propulsion necessary to hurl 3.5 million pounds through the Earth's atmosphere. A loud boom erupted as its engine compartment doors opened, releasing the beam of energy created. She felt her suit inflate to protect her body from the pressure of the 4g initial launch.

Pulling three to four g's was nothing new. Banking in her Navy F-22, she frequently pulled five or six. However, pulling three to four g's on your way to escape Earth's atmosphere in a solo-flight $10 billion atomic powered missile was another thing altogether. It was exhilarating!

"Aura. Stage 2 Engine Release in 3-2-1, mark."

Her fingers flew to the control panel nearby to complete the sequence used to initiate the Aura craft's second stage of its launch. "Stage 2 Engine Release," she replied, having flawlessly performed her duty. "Great! This means we are 27 seconds into launch." Sara thought to herself.

The power of atomic energy beams flowing through 16 propulsion nozzles behind her was impressive. But the acceleration she felt when all 48 fired was intense. Her breath became labored, so she tightened her diaphragm and grunted through it. Mission control cut off her mic so no one would hear her struggle. But they all knew what Sara was experiencing. The four g's had become 8 and the Aura's acceleration had jumped to over 5,000 miles per hour. She had about a half-minute left to endure the strain on her body before the Earth would finally let her go.

It stopped as suddenly as it had begun. Sara could no longer feel the Aura moving. There was a loud sound as all 48 thruster tubes were capped by Aura's AI flight system. A hiss of steam erupted in front of her as the ship fired its reverse thrusters to *slow her rate of acceleration. She made it. The mic light flickered back on as she heard Jim over her helmet speakers.*

"Aura, the Earth may have released you, but we've still got you here. Congratulations."

"Thank you, Mission Control. Sixty-two." Sara replied.

"Sixty-two!" Sally screamed as she pumped a fist in the air.

Most of that story is probably inaccurate. It was written by an outsider to space flight and the physics of atomic propulsion engines. But, there is one point on which we can all agree. You wouldn't send anyone into space without preparation. The margin for error is slim. And for that initial 62 miles, the Earth is applying multiple forces against you, trying to keep you here. Friction, gravity, temperature, wind shear, weather, and the human element of imperfection must all be overcome. The good thing is that they are known obstacles to achievement. So they Plan, Prepare and Practice. The idea is that Practice can lead to Proficiency and Proficiency can then be Performed under extreme environmental pressures.

In the Consultative Sales Model, achievement is realized when the decision maker understands that your proposal aligns with their needs scenario and agrees to move forward with a plan based upon necessary change. Not all obstacles can be known. And in a closing, the environmental pressures can be extreme. The model may be consultative, but the job is still sales. You've got to close, or it was all a waste of everyone's time.

Metaphors for battle are often used to describe sales. While the goal of Consultative Sales is to alleviate the adversarial relationship between buyer and seller; there are still many similarities to the modern-day battlefield. Most of them have to do with preparing for the unknown.

In his book, "Discipline Equals Freedom," former US Navy Seal Team Commander, Jocko Willink proposes that "with structure and a strict dedication to it, one can act with more efficiency and freedom." At first, the advice may sound contradictory. Concepts of structure and freedom seem at odds with one another. But, consider for a moment Captain Sara Summer's comment in the story above that she had flown her mission blindfolded. What that means is that her standard movements were so well planned and rehearsed that she no longer had to see to know she was performing. This level of structure actually provides the freedom for her mind to be available to think through any of the unknowns; because the known elements could be accomplished without thinking. A smoke-filled cockpit could be disastrous if a pilot couldn't automatically maneuver to the appropriate switches necessary for them to alleviate the cause for the smoke.

The good news is, just like in the space program, you can alleviate many of the known obstacles in your path with standardization. This structure provides you the freedom to think on the fly in order to address the things you could have never prepared for.

It begins with a standard format for the Summary Report. This report is the central document in Consultative Sales. It will become the vehicle by which you deliver your "case" to the client that they make a change based upon the Assessment and Analysis. But before you present the report, walk through the pathway to Performance. Organizations spend an extraordinary amount of time, money and energy training on the front end of sales. Role playing sales calls and repetition of products and services knowledge are a standard in any decent corporate sales training model. But, very rarely is time spent on closing the sale. If it is, it is often done in a way that dances around various iterations of the word, "No."

Why not set up the sale in such a way that there is not a "no" to contend with in the first place? Does it not make more sense to head into a sales scenario where you know this is what the client wants and needs? Sun

Tzu writes in "Art of War" that "Victorious warriors win first, and then go to war; while defeated warriors go to war first, and then seek to win." Going into the closing room without a winning plan is counter-productive.

It has already been established that Consultative Sales eliminates adversarial positions at the closing table. But, if you don't create a closing scenario then everyone loses. At this point, their organization is invested in the process; either through time, money, or both spent on the assessment process. You and your organization are clearly invested in the process. So, the "win" you are looking for is actually a win-win scenario. It's not one-sided. But the "battlefield" can still throw some pretty extreme and unexpected things at you. So, the only way for you to win first, then go to war, is by Planning, Preparing, and Practicing until you are Proficient enough to Perform an objective, compelling Summary Report for the client.

- Plan: Plan the layout for the Summary Report based upon the needs of the client organization.
- Preparation: Prepare for the delivery by soliciting the advice of senior members of your organization regarding the known issues of the client. Know

who will be present at the Summary Report delivery and consider their decision making process.

- Practice: Rehearse the Summary Report delivery until you no longer need it in front of you to present it.

- Proficiency: Webster's dictionary describes proficiency as the act of being well-rehearsed in an art, occupation, or branch of knowledge. Well-rehearsed is the result of practice. Preparation conveys an artful delivery. And knowledge of your client is the name of the game, given your occupation as a Consultant.

- Performance: The following is a guide for structuring and Performing the Summary Report based upon over a decade of Consultative Sales experience, across market sectors including banking/financial services, technology, aerospace, mining, utilities, entertainment, large non-profits, and government contracting.

Few things are more frustrating than seeing a sales person who has worked so hard to get a sale to the closing table, have the sale fall apart from lack of Preparation or Performance. The importance of Preparation has been well-covered in this chapter. So, now let's focus on Performance.

Like any goal, a good closing is accomplished in incremental steps. Each step is a component of a plan to use storytelling in order to paint a picture for the buyer as to how your solution solves the issues they are most concerned about. If a step is skipped, the likelihood of attaining the goal is diminished. In addition, each section reiterates the Consultative nature of the sale by keeping the focus of the presentation on the needs of the decision maker, rather than on the features of the solution.

Section 1. Executive Summary

The Executive Summary centers all parties on the basics of the current situation. Who are the two organizations or individuals involved? This can be as descriptive or as simplified as the case calls for, but it is often helpful to use this as an opportunity to factually begin to build the complexity of their situational need. This is also the opportunity for you to bring everyone back to the beginning by restating how this all started. What was the reason the decision maker agreed to an assessment in the first place?

Presentation: Reviewing the Executive Summary allows you to, in brief, remind everyone who is involved, why this is happening, what steps have been taken by everyone involved and what to expect as you move forward through the presentation. Remember Conscientious Leadership? It is the type of leadership necessary to facilitate a quality Summary Report delivery. You get to set this up in much the same way Sparrow set up making her point to Crow – by beginning with the end in mind. You know how this needs to end in order to create a win-win scenario. The buyer needs to agree to move forward with a plan to address their needs.

Begin the meeting by eliminating obstacles one by one. First, make certain everyone has blocked off the appropriate amount of time for the presentation. Second, set the tone for closing by asking if all decision makers for the organization are present. Finally, don't miss the opportunity to condition the affirmative. The purpose here is not some psychological manipulation designed to trick someone into buying into your proposal. It is the crucial convergence of meaning for the entire process. Simply put, make sure everyone is ready to explore findings from the assessment, identify challenges present within the organization, and be prepared to move forward with recommendations.

Section 2. Your Objectives

Every Assessment should begin with the question, "What are your goals for this assessment?" Their answer to that initial question should be included right here. This is also a great place to reiterate portions of their mission statement. You can also include any objectives you heard from other leaders and employees during your assessment. Make sure these are all their objectives and not your own. This is about them and their needs.

Presentation: This portion of the Summary Report is fairly straight-forward. However, precaution should be taken not to rush through it. Qualify each Objective by affirming that it is still valid and has not yet been addressed. For example:

OBJECTIVE 1: Create Lifetime Income During Retirement.

"Mr. Jones, you mentioned that one of the things you were most concerned about was running out of money during the withdrawal period of your retirement. So, a key objective of yours was to find a way to create a lifetime income throughout your retirement. Is that is still one of your primary objectives?"

"Yes."

"Great, we found a conservative and sensible way to address that for you."

Then, move on to Objective 2.

This step can take some time, but it is one of the most critical steps in your Summary Report delivery because it reiterates that everyone in the meeting is on the same page. It can also allow you to address any changes that may have taken place since your last meeting. It can also take a bit of creativity so you're not asking for affirmations six times in the same way. Practice and Preparation are critical.

You can also use this section as an opportunity to ensure nothing has changed within the organization which may change portions of your delivery.

Section 3. Findings Summary

Typically, this is the most lengthy and complex information to deliver. All of your Analysis will be included in this section. Sometimes, you'll be able to summarize it in a few paragraphs. Other times, it will take multiple pages.

<u>Presentation</u>: The more time you spend on this part, the better. Remember to use pictures and documentation gathered from the Assessment!

"Mrs. Banks, as you recall, your range of objectives met the prerequisite conditions for us to perform an Assessment. As it

turns out, that was a great decision on your part! Our findings support and emphasize validity of your concern and insight into your organization. We will spend the next few moments reviewing those with you."

Findings should include any leadership interviews conducted, information gathered, documents, policies, or processes reviewed. Often, one person will make a statement that truly ties everything together from Sections 2 & 3. Make it stand out. Especially if it is profound, like:

"A communications breakdown between all departments."

If there were instances of Frequency in your findings, put them in order of greatest to least under a "Common Issues" subheading. It provides evidential proof that issues exist within their current structure and helps to prioritize areas of greatest organizational need. You can also create powerful infographics to visually display Threading. Simple listing can be effective to display Inventory but be sure to include a summary that groups like items. Finally, save any reports generated using customized Reporting Tools for the end. Each time you present a Finding, it is vital that it is tied back to the Objectives of the buyer. For example:

"When you disclosed that you were worried about not knowing what BYOD technology was connecting to your network, we thought that was an insightful concern. Using diagnostic software, we ran a report showing every device that connected to your network. We then eliminated those with IP addresses belonging to the technology owned by your company. Our list shows that in a period of 1 week, 37 mobile phones and 6 tablets connected to your network."

Section 4. Our Recommendations

Here is the opportunity for you to provide solutions to the issues their organization is experiencing. Make sure to order your Recommendations in the same order as the Frequency of the organizational needs defined in the "Common Issues" or "Findings" portion of the Summary Report. One key feature here is not to include pricing, yet. Simply lay out the Recommendation and how it solves their Issues and Objectives.

<u>Presentation</u>:

"First, we recommend a clearly defined Social Media strategy. Statistics show that over 90% of buyers research Social Media before reaching a buying decision and your organization definitely needs to show up to that party. This also addresses your Objectives of reaching a younger female target-market while taking into consideration your decrease in annual Marketing budget; since most social media users are females between the ages of 18 – 35 and social media platforms are free to use. As we pointed out previously, this was also something several specialists in your Product Development department felt strongly about. Does this sound like a strategy you can get on board with?"

Notice how the Recommendation clearly defines why it makes sense relative to their needs scenario. It ties in Objectives, possibly a bit of Frequency Analysis from your Findings, and even includes a relevant supporting statistic. At the end, the presenter also made sure to gain buy-in to the recommendation from the decision maker.

Section 5. Proposed Execution

One of the benefits of the Consultative Sales Model is that it opens the door for multiple solutions. Depending upon your marketable output, this can feel overwhelming and costly to a decision maker. Proposing solutions utilizing a phased approach delivered over time enables you to tackle the area of greatest need (therefore greatest pain) first, while also establishing a path to address other Objectives and needs outlined in the report.

Perhaps the most interesting thing this does is set your organization up as the project manager for delivering the phases based upon the timeline mechanism you choose. Sales pipelines are one of the most frequently reviewed metrics of a sales person. What are your long-term and short-term opportunities? Most often, this list is populated based on a hunch. It involves the marketer having to "guesstimate" the readiness or willingness of someone else to make a buying decision.

A Proposed Execution is beneficial in two ways. It takes out the guesswork regarding timeframes; while actually allowing you to be the one to recommend when they should make a buying decision. Second, it creates a revenue pipeline built not only from new clients, but from existing ones. In other words, it literally doubles (at a minimum) your earnings potential as a marketer.

After presenting the timeline to the decision maker ask them if that timeline is reasonable based on their schedule. Make adjustments as necessary and document any changes made to the timelines on the Summary Report.

Section 6. Investment Plan

If you've done your job right, this sale is no longer about them buying something from your organization. It is about investing in their own organization in order to resolve known issues and resolve organizational needs scenarios. Calling it an Investment Plan is neither tongue-in-cheek or deceptive. It is often helpful to preface the Investment Plan by reminding them of that.

"This Investment Plan represents the best method for ABC Corporation to accomplish (state relevant objective) by eliminating (state relevant issue/finding) by investing $(state amount) back into your organization."

Section 7. Signatures

The best time to get a signature is at the time of proposal. That is true for both Traditional Sales and Consultative Sales. The difference is in how you get it done.

In Section 5 of the Summary Report, you laid out an Execution Strategy for implementing the plan necessary to address their situational needs and objectives. That plan had a start date. The best closing option you can use is to rely on that by simply stating:

"Your signature is required for us to be ready to meet your Execution Timeline as stated in this Summary Report."

Chapter Seven : Key Points

- Plan. Prepare. Practice. Proficiency. Perform.
- Presenting a Summary Report should be a well-planned and practiced process
- Achievement can only be accomplished if the decision maker understands that your proposed solutions align with their needs scenario
- It was a waste of everyone's time if you don't close
- Structure and discipline add to the freedom in which you operate
- "Win first, then go to war."
- The win you are looking for is actually a win-win.
- Good delivery of a Summary Report paints a picture for the decision maker.
- Steps for Performing a Summary Report:
  o Executive Summary
  o Your Objectives
  o Findings Summary
  o Our Recommendations
  o Proposed Execution
  o Investment Plan
  o Signatures

Chapter 8

In Closing

When I first got started down this journey, an older gentleman approached me and asked me what I did. I hadn't quite figured it all out yet. So, I abruptly replied, "I sell to sales people."

He offered to buy me a drink.

Why is that? What is it about the nature of sales that has created such an adversarial dichotomy between buyer and seller? Clearly the two relationships rely on one another in order to accomplish their individual goals. A buyer is in search of a suitable product or service. A marketer is looking to resolve various needs scenarios with their marketable output. The two should be symbiotic in their relationship. But they're not.

As a matter of fact, as a society, we often treat sales people the way humans in the Walking Dead treat their zombie counterparts. We create barriers (literal and figurative), barricade ourselves behind layers and various forms of protection, duck around corners whenever one is near, and when all else fails, we run in the opposite direction!

But, at the heart of it all are people who typically possess the following characteristics:

- Empathetic
- Fun
- Outgoing
- Charming
- Engaging
- Driven

That hardly sounds like the plight of humanity!

Now, when anyone asks me what I do, I tell them that I'm lucky enough to wake up every day and work with some of the most passionate, fun, driven labor force on the planet: Sales People! My goal is to disrupt the sales training industry by breaking apart a century-old sales model and rebuilding a sales culture based on the needs & expectations of today's buyer. The end result is bigger sales, better customers and sales people who love their job!

To put it mildly, I LOVE Sales People!

So, it is my genuine hope that this book can help bridge the gap between buyer and seller by eliminating abusive sales practices and creating the realization that Sales People don't deserve to be shunned. The Traditional Sales model is to blame! But, before we demonize something, undeservedly, it makes sense to stop long enough to recognize that it was once effective. Where Sales as an industry has failed is in our collective lack of response to over a century of change.

I invite you to imagine a world where Sales People are viewed as problem solvers, and where they act as consultants to their clients and prospects.

I have.

And I'm tirelessly devoted to disrupting the century-old paradigm that has pitted us as adversaries to one another in favor of one where we work together to achieve amazing things!

Please feel free to reach out to me with your own questions, comments or ideas on how we can work together to fix something statistics prove is broken. I would consider it an honor.

J Michael can be reached by email at:
salesgrinds@gmail.com

References

Covey, S. (1989) "*The 7 Habits of Highly Effective People*"

Gladwell, M. (2018) "*Outliers*"

Tracy, B. (1985) "*The Psychology of Selling*"

Tzu, S. (~500 BC) "*The Art of War*"

Willink, J. (2017) "*Discipline Equals Freedom*"

Websites Referenced:

www.Forbes.com

www.Hubspot.com

www.Spotio.com

www.TrainingMagazine.com

www.LinkedIn.com

www.CrunchBase.com (formerly Compare Metrics)

www.HBR.org

THE AUTHOR:

J Michael Smith is a lucky husband to one hot wife and a proud father to 5 amazing kids. And, he is sold out on sales people! J Michael spent 20 years amid the intertwined worlds of consulting and sales. During that time, he was struck by the contrast that exists between the broken nature of the Traditional Sales model and the amazing effort and dedication of sales people forced to adhere to it. Buyers have changed. Buyers' needs have changed. And the sales industry has done little to respond. This Handbookguide is just one of the ways he is working to change that. Learn more at www.thehandbookguide.com.

THE ILLUSTRATOR:

David Myers is a devoted husband and a really cool Dad. He and the author first became friends on the UNCW Men's Swimming & Diving team where they were frequently separated on bus trips so no one had to suffer under their rendition of Aretha Franklin's "Respect". When his head wasn't in the water, it was in books, studying art at the University of North Carolina in Wilmington. David is now an artist based out of North Carolina and works in many different types of media. His work can be viewed at www.artisservant.blogspot.com – and in this book!

By the way... this is us!
(David Myers as "Sgt. Grimm" & J Michael Smith as "Mike")

Made in the USA
Lexington, KY
08 December 2019

58265918R00097